Rocky Mountain National Park Trail Guide

Rocky Mountain National Park Trail Guide

By Erik Nilsson

World Publications

P.O. Box 366, Mountain View, CA 94042

second printing, May 1983

Library of Congress C.I.P. Number 78-362

ISBN 0-89037-098-2

To the memory of Thomas Byron Hawkins—"Hawkeye." I loved him like a brother and as much as he loved the mountains about which this book has been written. "All men must have adventures."

Contents

Acknowledgements

It is within the confines of this short space that an author is allowed to express, often inadequately, his appreciation for the assistance offered by friends and acquaintances in writing a book. I now find myself wanting to express that gratitude to all who, in one way or another, have made this book possible.

First, I would like to extend thanks and recognition to David Noe for his helpful advice on certain trails of the park. His exact measurements of trail mileages has allowed me to present updated statistics on campsite mileage and locations. If this book is successful part of the responsibility will be his.

Thanks also to park naturalist Dwight Hamilton and all the people at park headquarters who reviewed my manuscript and made suggestions and corrections. Though he may not have thought I was really writing a book on the park, he offered his time and assistance, even putting up with my frequent phone calls.

I must also express my gratitude to two good friends and dart-throwing fanatics. Thanks to Jerry Read for his knowledgeable advice concerning problems I encountered with the graphics, and to Tom Post for pulling off several darkroom marathons in preparing the photographs.

I would additionally like to thank several people whose names I either never knew or have forgotten: hikers along the trail with whom I've struck up conversations, and customers at the Outpost in Fort Collins who have hiked the park and imparted bits and pieces of their experiences to me.

Finally, I extend thanks to my brother, Dr. Tom Nilsson, and my close friend and confidant, Scott Bowie. Tom and I have hiked many of the park's trails together and his companionship has made those trips that much better. From our Stead's Ranch and Wind River days to the present we've shared a lot. Thank you Tom.

Scott Bowie, presently and no doubt permanently of Aspen, Colorado, was the unknowing catalyst for the inception of this book. Regardless of my untried merit as a writer, he made me want to try—an act of friendship I'll not forget. We too have shared. Elk Tooth was only yesterday and it was a thousand years ago.

Introduction

Rocky Mountain National Park became this nation's tenth national park in January 1915, when President Wilson signed the bill proposing its creation. It was the culmination of years of effort by national as well as local champions of conservation. Among these conservationists, Estes Park pioneers were the most prominent. Enos Mills, the park's most influential proponent, sought to preserve this area of more than four hundred square miles for the enjoyment of future generations. We, today, as well as our children, owe a debt of thanks to people like Mills for their foresight and concern. Those who travel by foot trails or highways among these mountains can enjoy a kinship with those early naturalists—a common appreciation for the simple beauty this national park offers its visitors. It was this same beauty that drew the park's previous inhabitants, the Ute and Arapaho Indians. Many of the local place-names are derived from Indian words for the mountains, rivers, and valleys. If each of us emulated the reverence for the land that its original inhabitants held, the job of the park ranger would be considerably easier.

Located roughly sixty miles northwest of Denver, Rocky Mountain National Park (RMNP) is near two main resort areas. The first is Estes Park, where the park headquarters is located. From the east, the visitor can travel U.S. Route 34 through Big Thompson Canyon from Loveland, U.S. Route

36 up the North Saint Vrain Canyon, or Colorado Route 7 via the South Saint Vrain. The latter two originate at Lyons in the foothills north of Boulder. Each of these scenic routes has its particular appeal, especially for those making their first trip to the mountains. Across the continental divide on the western slope is another resort area at the town of Grand Lake, situated on U.S. Route 34 north of its juncture with U.S. Route 40 at the town of Granby. Grand Lake is a prime vacation spot for boating enthusiasts, for it is one of three scenic bodies of water in the area. Just south of Grand Lake are Shadow Mountain Lake and Lake Granby.

Trail Ridge Road connects Grand Lake and Estes Park. It is not only the highest paved road in the country, with its highest point 12,183 feet above sea level, but also one of the most spectacular scenic drives in any national park. Completed in 1932, it replaced Fall River Road, the original route connecting the two towns. The eastern part of the road began at the western end of Horseshoe Park and proceeded along Fall River to Fall River Pass. At this point on Trail Ridge Road, there is presently a restaurant, a gift shop, and the national park Alpine Visitor Center. When Fall River Road opened in 1920, it was a true challenge to the Model T's that traveled it. The western part of Fall River Road took essentially the same route as the present-day Trail Ridge Road.

Sometime after Trail Ridge was opened, the old road was closed to vehicle travel and fell into disrepair. But on July 1, 1968, it was reopened to one-way traffic, going uphill to the west, and once again offers park visitors an alternate scenic route from Estes Park to Grand Lake. However, because of its sharp switchbacks trailer traffic is not allowed. Model T's, however, are welcome.

A third highway into the park is the Bear Lake Road. This accounts, in part, for the popularity of the lakes and mountains of the Bear Lake/Glacier Gorge area. Unlike Trail Ridge and Fall River roads, Bear Lake Road is kept open in the winter. With the increasing interest in cross-country skiing, Bear Lake and vicinity is seeing more winter visitors each year. Not long ago even seeing more than a handful of snowshoers would have been quite a coincidence.

Rocky Mountain National Park headquarters is located about 2.5 miles west of Estes Park on U.S. Route 34, a bit more than halfway between town and the Beaver Meadows park entrance. During the summer season it is open from 8:00 a.m. to 9:00 p.m. every day, and offers a variety of books, pamphlets, and maps on the area, as well as regularly scheduled movies about the park. Information is also available regarding camping permits, guided nature hikes, and campfire talks. This book will answer questions the visitor may have regarding places to hike, specific camping areas, proper equipment, and general safety rules.

HOW TO USE THIS BOOK

This book has been written as a guide for hikers and campers in Rocky Mountain National Park. The book begins with a discussion of the history of the area, to give the visitor some idea of RMNP's colorful past. Next is a chapter on natural history, with an overview of the geologic history, and the flora and fauna of RMNP. For the novice backpacker, a chapter has been included on equipment, its selection and use. There is treatment of the subjects of proper conditioning, pacing oneself on a hike, and first aid, including physical disorders associated with mountaineering and safety. The chapter on park regulations has been reproduced from material supplied by the National Park Service.

Part three begins with a discussion of topographical maps, and contains the appropriate reproduced sections of the United States Geological Survey 1:62500 map of RMNP. Campsites are marked with code letters on these chapter maps, and trailheads are indicated. Additionally, the text of each chapter is preceded by a list of the specific 7.5-minute series maps for the campsites discussed, as well as the cross-country zones in that area. The entire list of East and West District campsites appears in Appendix A.

Although the maps in this book will assist the hiker, it is best to obtain 7.5-minute series maps for the area in which you intend to hike. These maps are usually available at park headquarters or U.S. Geological Survey offices for around $1.25 per map. If you would like to secure maps before your visit, you can do so by writing for a map order form. The address is: Central Region—Map Distribution, United States Geological Survey, Federal Center Building, No. 41, Denver, Colorado 80225.

As a general rule, this book avoids discussion of hiking time, either one-way or round trip. The reason is that time will vary considerably, depending on the level of conditioning of the hiker. To determine hiking time, it is advisable to take a few hikes of varying length and terrain. Using your wristwatch and the trail mileages recorded in this book, establish what a comfortable pace is for you on easy as well as steeper trails. An average pace is approximately two miles per hour.

Some of the lakes and mountains in this guidebook do not have established trails leading to them. Consult the maps in each chapter to determine the trails for the areas you wish to visit. The distances to many lakes and mountains for which there are trails have been measured exactly, but appear in the book rounded off to the nearest tenth of a mile. Areas lacking established routes are listed with close approximations of the mileage. Such distances will vary slightly with the route chosen, but are a reasonable guide to distance traveled. Overall vertical rise in elevation for any given trail can be determined by subtracting the elevation of the starting point from that of the proposed destination.

This book also avoids discussion of technical rock climbing in the park. An adequate treatment of the sport, as practiced in the Estes Park region, may be found in some of the books mentioned in the Bibliography.

In conclusion, it should be pointed out that the author has not climbed every mountain, walked every trail, or visited every lake in this park. However, this book is the result of the author's own experiences, coupled with the insights of park rangers and naturalists noted in the acknowledgments. It is hoped that the result is an informative guide to the trails and scenic features of Rocky Mountain National Park, as well as a useful outline of general camping equipment and safety.

Rocky Mountain National Park

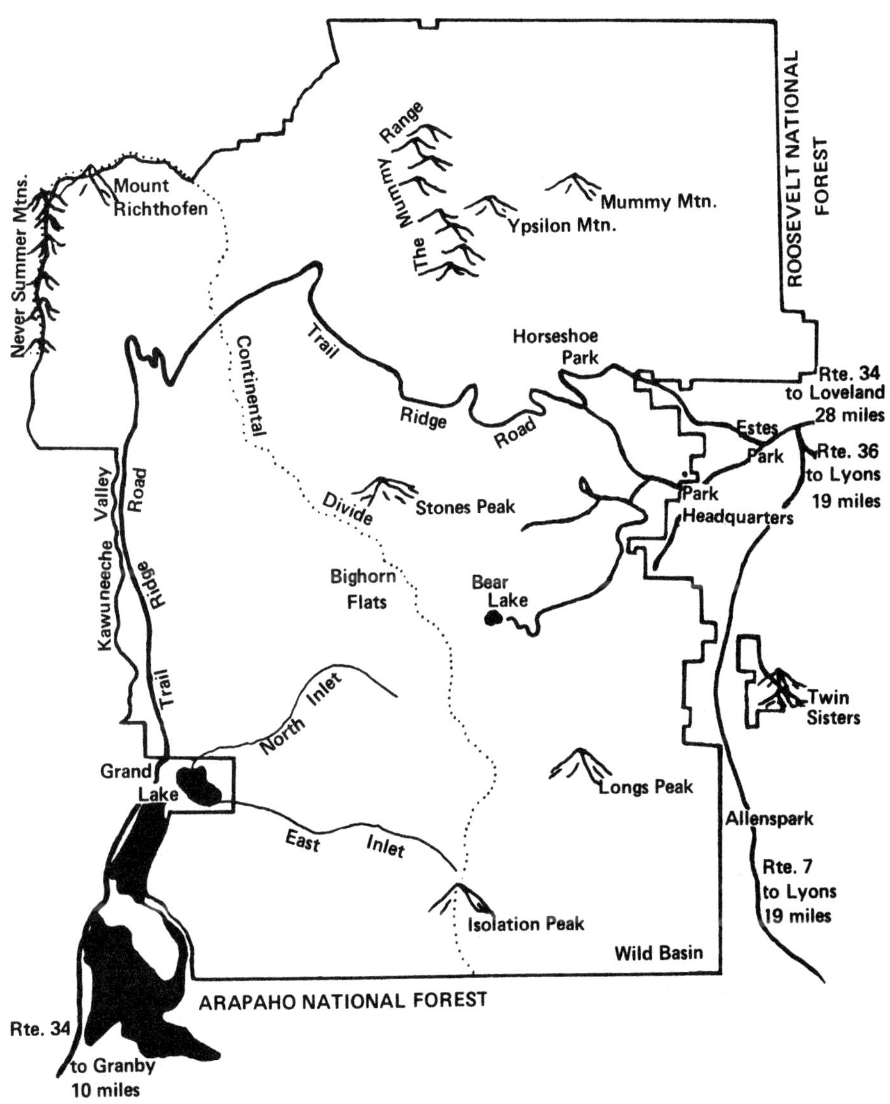

CHIEFS HEAD
GLACIER GORGE
McHENRYS PEAK
THATCHTOP
TAYLOR GLACIER
TAYLOR PEAK

OTIS PEAK
HALLETT PEAK
TYNDALL GLACIER
FLATTOP MTN.
ODESSA GORGE
NOTCHTOP
KNOBTOP
GABLETOP

(Preceding page) The Front Range as seen from Eagle Cliff. Moraine Park and the Bear Lake Road are in the valley below. The entire length of the horizon is part of the continental divide. (Photograph courtesy of the National Park Service.)

Part One

Background on the Park

Chapter 1

History of the Park

Tombstone, Arizona; Deadwood, South Dakota; Dodge City, Kansas; the Comstock Lode; the Black Hills; Estes Park, Colorado. Did you say Estes Park, Colorado? Although Estes Park has a familiar name, few people think of it as having the colorful history of places like Tombstone, Arizona. Though Estes Park had no infamous sheriffs or boot hills (cemeteries), no great Indian battlegrounds or army forts, and no huge mining claims, it nonetheless had a colorful history. If you are acquainted with this past, it is all the more interesting to tour the area around Rocky Mountain National Park.

THE ARAPAHO INDIANS

The earliest inhabitants of this area, about whom little is known, were the Paleo-Indians. It is thought that they entered the park area as early as 7,500 years ago to hunt game during the summer. But they probably vacated these hunting grounds 5,800 years ago, with the cooling of the climate and the recurrence of glacial activities.

There is disagreement as to when the Arapaho Indians, who called themselves *Inunaina* ("Our People"), first set foot in this region, as well as where they came from. They are an Algonquian people, whose language is related to that of the Cheyennes. The Arapaho probably traveled the plains from the East and eventually reached the mountains of

Colorado in the early 1700s. From that time until the middle 1800s, they visited the high country of what later became Rocky Mountain National Park in spring through fall, retreating to the plains for the winter. Estes Park was apparently popular with the Arapaho, since it was filled with game, grazing land for the horses, and timber for firewood and tipi poles.

The Ute, the perennial enemies of the Arapaho, also frequented the area that became Rocky Mountain National Park, but rarely east of the continental divide. Normally they ventured only to the Grand Lake and western slope areas. The trail from Estes Park to Grand Lake, known as the Ute Trail, was used by the Arapaho, who called it the Childs Trail. This name derived from an Arapaho word meaning "where the children walked," implying that the trail was so steep in places that children had to get off the horses and walk. This trail originates in Beaver Meadows, just west of the park entrance of the same name, and extends up to timberline and along present-day Trail Ridge Road.

If you travel the old Fall River Road, which originates on the western end of Horseshoe Park, you will retrace the route of the oldest trail in the park region. This was known as the Dog Trail, and received its name from the Indians' use of dogs to help carry possessions up to Fall River Pass and the junction of the Dog and Childs trails.

The Arapaho had more than just Utes to contend with in the early days. In 1914, a two-week pack trip was undertaken to tour the future Rocky Mountain National Park area. Among the explorers were two old Arapaho Indians, who came down from their reservation in Wyoming especially for this trip. They spoke of the Indian history of this region, where they had lived as boys, and pointed out where great battles had ensued with the Utes, Shoshone, and Apache. According to these two Indian guides, in 1855 an Apache war party encountered an Arapaho camp near Moraine Park, and had a running battle all the way through Beaver Meadows to the north. To this day, there are remnants of the stone fortifications constructed by the beseiged Apaches on a rock outcropping near Beaver Meadows. Rock piles were originally stacked four feet high at strategic points on top of the outcrop. Unfortunately, a local settler utilized this rock for the foundation of his home, and today little of the original fort remains.

Imagine fifty cornered Apaches furiously mounting one boulder on top of another, as swarms of Arapaho parade back and forth below, waving decorated *coup sticks* and shields, and shouting to each other.* The falsetto tremolos of each tribe's war songs are sung as attacks are initiated and repulsed. Arrows are launched and war clubs swung in hand-to-hand fighting. The Great Spirit is called upon by the holy men of each tribe to help bring victory.

The Apaches eventually sneaked out in the black of night and made an escape. According to the old Indians on the pack trip, the Arapaho chief decided not to pursue the intruders as they fled, since they had accomplished their purpose. One of the essential elements of Indian warfare was that a tribe had only to demonstrate bravery against an enemy, but did not need to annihilate them. The latter was taught to the Indians by their encounters with the U.S. Army, and was learned well by the time of Little Bighorn, scene of Custer's last stand.

Many of the place-names in Rocky Mountain National Park derive from Arapaho words. The Indian method of choosing names for mountains, lakes, parks, and rivers differed markedly from that of white settlers in the Estes Park/Grand Lake area. The Indians felt that geographical points should commemorate events that had occurred there, or certain characteristics of the place. White settlers more often chose names to honor local residents or original explorers of a region.

For instance, Longs Peak derives its name from Stephen Long, an army officer who led an expedition into Colorado in 1820. However, the Indians called Longs the "Two Guides," referring to Longs and neighboring Mount Meeker. Bierstadt Lake was named after Albert Bierstadt, the famous

**Coup sticks* looked like small shepherd staffs, and were covered with buffalo fur. They were used to touch an enemy, the greatest show of courage in warfare. That is how feathers were awarded to wear in headdresses or in the hair.

western painter. The Arapaho name for the same place was Hanging Lake. Viewed from the Flattop Mountain trail, the lake seems perched on top of the Bierstadt Moraine. Many Arapaho names in the park have survived translation. Among them are Nokhu Crags, from a phrase meaning "the eagles nest," and Kawuneeche Valley, the word for "coyote" and Tonahutu, the word for "big meadows."

THE ESTES RANCH

By 1859, when Joel Estes entered the park that now bears his name, the Arapaho had left for good, and a new chapter in the history of the area had begun. Joel Estes had come to Colorado from Missouri as part of the initial wave of fortune hunters in the original Colorado gold rush. A decade before, he had done the same thing in California, and had been lucky. This time, however, he took up ranching instead of mining. It was on a trip into the mountains, looking for summer grazing land, that he discovered the beautiful basin the Arapahoes called "The Circle." Estes, taken with its beauty, moved there in 1863, and started ranching there with his family and that of one of his sons.

The cold, snowy winter of 1865-66 convinced Estes that a warmer climate was more to his liking. In April 1866, the Estes clan left the region for New Mexico, and sold their property for a pittance. Accounts vary, but it seems the Estes holdings were traded for a yearling steer and about fifty dollars cash.

Estes's claim changed hands the next year, and became the property of Griff Evans, a Welchman of jovial disposition. He became the original guest ranch operator of the area, bedding and feeding the trickle of park visitors, many of whom came to see and climb Longs Peak. Climbing this mountain became popular with adventure-seekers ever since John Wesley Powell's first recorded ascent in 1868. By 1873, several climbing parties had made the climb. The first woman to make the ascent was Anna Dickinson, who reached the summit with the Hayden Geographical Survey Party on September 13, 1873.

In 1866, a reflector telescope 16 feet in diameter and 280 feet in length was mounted on the summit of Longs Peak to observe the course of the first rocket to the moon. Though this may sound peculiar, it was greeted enthusiastically by science-fiction fans of the day, who read, with great delight, this fictional scenario in Jules Verne's *From the Earth to the Moon.*

LORD DUNRAVEN BUYS ESTES PARK

At Christmas, 1872, an Englishman came to the Estes Park area to hunt. He became entranced by the natural beauty he saw, and excited at the prospect of so much game. He returned again in 1873, and casually announced to his traveling companion that he wished to acquire the entire Estes Park area as a private hunting preserve. The man was Windham Thomas Wyndam-Quin, Fourth Earl of Dunraven, Viscount of Mount Earl and Adare—Lord Dunraven for short. Lord Dunraven was a handsome, young English nobleman who possessed great property and wealth. He also had quite an adventurous spirit. He loved horses and was reputed to be one of the best steeplechasers in England. He had been a foreign correspondent for a London newspaper in 1867, during a war in Abyssinia (Ethiopia). It may have been then that Lord Dunraven first heard tales of hunting in the Colorado mountains, as one of his fellow war correspondents had been to Colorado the year before. That man was Sir Henry M. Stanley, who four years later in Central Africa uttered the famous words, "Doctor Livingstone, I presume?" The previous year, Stanley had borrowed fifty dollars to construct a raft, and floated out of Colorado down the Platte River.

Lord Dunraven was a man who usually got what he wanted, and he desperately wanted Estes Park. This would be his personal domain when he visited America, a place that, under his auspices, would be spared the plow and the ax. To that end, he enlisted the help of Griff Evans, his host when he visited Estes in 1872. He also chose a fellow Englishman, Theodore Whyte, to act as his agent in buying the land. Whyte was a hunter and had trapped professionally with the Hudson Bay Company in Canada.

In 1874, Estes Park Company, Ltd., popularly known as

Estes Park in the early 1900s. The town has changed but not the view. The general store at left center announces its wares as "Baled Hay & Grain & Camper's Supplies." The dirt road at left center is Elkhorn Avenue, the main street. (Photograph courtesy of Denver Public Library, Western History Department.)

the English Company, was formed, and the task of securing title to thousands of acres began. The methods employed in circumventing the Homestead Law were of questionable legality at best. According to that law, no person could claim more than 160 acres. Whyte enlisted a veritable army of Denver drunks and unemployed drifters to sign homestead claims in the Estes Park region. Many of them probably didn't even know where Estes Park was located. After the claims were "legally" filed, Whyte dispersed money to all who had claimed property, and title was transfered to the English Company. In several instances fictitious names were used when the supply of willing conspirators ran low.

By various means, Lord Dunraven managed to gain control over about 15,000 acres of land. It was common knowledge that the English Company had employed illegal tactics, but apparently that was less obnoxious to local people than the Lord's general attitude. When his land company was formed, the *Rocky Mountain News* in Denver carried Dunraven's announcement that Estes Park was off limits, with admittance by invitation only. This upper-class arrogance incensed the egalitarian-minded pioneers, causing a fair amount of ill will toward Lord Dunraven and his company.

Most notable among this anti-Dunraven group was a local settler named James Nugent. He was a colorful man, right out of the so-called pages of the old west known as Rocky Mountain Jim, and stories about him are endless. Very little of what Rocky Mountain Jim claimed as his background can be verified. But even if one-tenth of these experiences really happened, he led an utterly flamboyant existence. He said variously that he was a Canadian son of a British officer, a Missouri farmer who had fought with Quantrell's Raiders in Kansas, a former employee of the Hudson Bay Company and the American Fur Company, and even stated that he was a nephew of Confederate Civil War General P. G. T. Beauregard. He hired himself out in Estes Park as a hunting, fishing, and mountaineering guide. His face had been badly scarred by a bear attack, but his "good side" was said to be handsome and he had a way with women he met. He had long, blond, curly hair, and was quite articulate when reciting poetry of his own composition. Lord Dunraven's personal physician, a Dr. Kingsley, suggested that the name Rocky Mountain Jim was appropriate considering the "attitude of his lies."

Rocky Mountain Jim and Lord Dunraven mixed like fire and gasoline. A feud began quickly between Jim and one of Dunraven's men, Griff Evans. An associate of Evans named Hague had been run off at gunpoint by Rocky Mountain Jim following a dispute over a woman. A short time later, as Jim was passing near Evans's cabin on horseback, Evans and Hague walked out, and Evans shot Jim out of the saddle with a double-barreled shotgun. His wounds proved fatal, and he died in the Collins House Hotel in Fort Collins ten weeks later.

This incident, along with increased resistance to Lord Dunraven's private playground, began changing the nobleman's outlook on his land holdings. He had not moved to Colorado, and only occasionally retreated there. He became

Steads Ranch, formerly called Spragues Hotel, as it appeared circa 1915. Steads was a classic example of the hotels in and around the park from the late 1800s until the 1950s. The setting is Moraine Park, just off the Bear Lake Road, near the present-day site of the Moraine Park campground. (Photograph courtesy of Denver Public Library, Western History Department.)

increasingly pessimistic about operating his paradise from afar through his agent, Whyte. The following excerpts from his memoirs indicate he knew what was coming:

> After a time people began to wander in. . . . It became evident that we were not to be left monarchs of all we surveyed. Folks were drifting in prospecting, fossicking, preempting, making claims; so we prepared for civilization. Made a better road, bought a saw-mill at San Francisco, hauled the machinery in, felled trees, and built a wooden hotel, and did pretty well with a Chinese cook who could make venison and anything else out of a bogged cow beef. . . .
>
> People came in disputing claims, kicking up rows; exorbitant land taxes got into arrears; we were in constant litigation. The show could not be managed from home, and we were in danger of being frozen out. So we sold what we could get and cleared out, and I have never been there since.*

*Louisa Ward Arps and Elinor Eppich Kingery, *High Country Names* (Denver: The Colorado Mountain Club, 1966), pp. 54-55.

Lord Dunraven's dream of owning a mountain retreat lasted only thirty-three years until 1907. The land baron of Estes Park died in London in 1926 at the age of eighty-five.

EARLY HOTELS

So ended in 1907 another chapter in Estes Park history. By that time, the region was well established as a tourist attraction and many guest ranches and hotels had been constructed. More would soon follow. Guests stayed at these rustic retreats for the same reasons people visit Estes Park today: to enjoy horseback riding, sight-seeing, mountaineering, picnicking, and the crisp, clean mountain air. Among the original hotels were Steads Ranch, Brinwood Hotel, Spragues Lodge, Fern Lake Lodge, Forest Canyon Inn, Fall River Ranch, Longs Peak Inn, Copeland Lake Lodge, Phantom Valley Ranch, Wind River Ranch, and Horseshoe Inn. Frank Lloyd Wright designed the latter, and like other hotels of the region, it blended well with the surroundings, rather than detracting from them.

The Longs Peak Inn, built in 1906, was owned by perhaps the most famous Estes Park resident, Enos Abijah Mills (1870-1922). Enos Mills, more than any other person, helped establish the movement to get national park status for this region. Mills was a boy of fifteen when his family moved to Estes Park from Kansas, and he immediately took up mountaineering. Three years later, in 1888, he became a summer guide for the increasing number of visitors who wanted to climb Longs Peak. During the winter he worked as a snow observer for the Colorado Department of Engineers. He wandered the mountains alone to measure the snow pack depth in order to determine the amount of spring runoff. It was on these trips, as guide and snow observer, that he accumulated his vast knowledge about the flora and fauna of the area. He later recorded this knowledge in sixteen books on wildlife, and drew on it when he acted as a naturalist lecturer.

Mills decided to purchase a guest lodge near Longs Peak as both a base camp for climbers, and a mountain retreat where he could prepare his lectures and books. In order to secure the needed money, he worked several winters as a miner in Butte, Montana, until he was able to buy the homestead property of Elkanah Lamb in 1902. Elkanah Lamb (1832-1915) was a preacher turned mountaineering guide. He must have been a striking man, 6'4" and very active. He had come to the mountains to conduct a town-to-town ministry. Eventually he became a guide, charging five dollars per person, and built his Longs Peak House in Tahosa Valley to the east of Longs Peak. He once remarked that if people wouldn't pay him to guide them spiritually, he would have them pay to be guided up Longs. Mills's place was called Longs Peak House, and he operated it under that name until a fire devastated it. In 1906, he rebuilt it as the Longs Peak Inn. Enos Mills's guiding years, 1888 to 1905, concluded for the most part when he rebuilt his mountain hotel. He transferred his guide duties to professional guides in his employ, and turned his attention to writing and operating the Longs Peak Inn.

THE PARK BECOMES A REALITY

In 1909, Mills first got the idea of having this country he loved preserved in its natural state as a national park. Thirty-nine years before, Yellowstone National Park had been created, as had several others since that time. The original idea was to name it Estes National Park, but for various reasons, the consensus of opinion shifted to Rocky Mountain National Park. Enos Mills utilized his ability as a lecturer as well as his knowledge of the area to promote the idea of the park and the need for conservation. Six years after the idea first came to Mills, he participated in the dedication ceremony of Rocky Mountain National Park on September 4, 1915. This simple ceremony took place in Horseshoe Park.

The boundaries of the park later expanded in 1929, when the Never Summer Mountains were added. The headwaters of the North Fork of the Colorado River are located in this region. Traditionally, the Colorado had been called the Grand River (thus, Grand Lake, Grand Ditch, Grand Junction, Grand Canyon, etc.). A powerful U.S. congressman, Edward F. Taylor, was spokesman for a small group of people who felt that the Colorado was a more appropriate name for this mighty river. The people of Arizona were furious and those in Utah, indignant. Utah argued that since the Green River, which joined the Grand, was the longer water course, the Grand River should be considered part of the Green River. But since the Grand Canyon was in Arizona, Arizonians felt that changing the name of the river was inappropriate in light of the fame of the Grand Canyon. Since the U.S. Board on Geographic Names refused to sit in the middle of such a squabble, the matter went to Congress. Taylor won, and on July 25, 1921, President Harding signed the bill changing the name of the Grand to the Colorado River.

F.O. STANLEY

Among the fascinating characters that Estes Park has seen, Freelan O. Stanley is one of the most interesting. After Lord Dunraven gave up his plans in Estes, Stanley bought considerable land and created the incredible Stanley Hotel in 1909. The Stanley Hotel was a wonder—no luxury was spared. It was lit by electricity (from the first Estes Park power plant, which Stanley built), and cost over half a million dollars to build. The Stanley Hotel, still in operation today, is a wonderful link with the history of Estes Park.

F. O. Stanley was a resourceful inventor. His doctors had given him one year to live, when he came to Estes Park from Massachusetts in 1903. The physicians' prophesy of death did not come true until 1940, when Stanley finally succumbed at ninety-one. Among his many inventions was the Stanley Dry Plate, used in photography, the patent for which was sold to Eastman Kodak. He also invented the remarkable Stanley Steamer automobile. He had arrived in Estes Park with this steam-powered horseless carriage, and soon got the idea of operating an automobile stage line from Lyons to Estes Park. After personally improving what later became U.S. Route 36, Stanley built a fleet of four twelve-passenger steamers and, by 1907, was in business. After the completion of the Stanley Hotel, guests were personally picked up at the train depot in Lyons, and brought to the hotel in these amazing vehicles.

The dedication of Rocky Mountain National Park on September 4, 1915. Enos Mills, the man principally responsible for the park's formation, is second from the left. To the right of Mills is F. O. Stanley, inventor of the Stanley Steamer automobile and founder of the Stanley Hotel. To the right of Stanley is Edward F. Taylor, the Colorado congressman responsible for changing the name of the Grand River to the Colorado River. (Photograph courtesy of Denver Public Library, Western History Department.)

Stanley had one curious eccentricity, ironic in an inventor of automobiles. He refused to drive backward. To avoid having to do so, he installed a rotating floor in his garage so he could always leave and enter in forward gear. If any readers of this book have any insight into this bizarre predilection, I'd like to hear about it. I'm still trying to figure it out.

Though there have been many Estes Park characters whose lives warrant mention, this is unfortunately impossible in this work. Consult the Bibliography for some good books on local history.

THE ORIGIN OF PARK NAMES

This brief history will conclude with a look at some local place-names and their origins. The history of Estes Park is sketched by these names–some after people, others based on geographical features.

Lucius Fairchild, for whom Fairchild Mountain was named, was three times the governor of Wisconsin and was a Civil War veteran. He was made U. S. Minister to Spain by President Hayes in 1880, and was elected commander in chief of the Grand Army of the Republic.

Cabin Creek in Wild Basin is named for the remnants of a stone cabin near its bank. This was reputedly the solitary winter quarters of the famous mountain man and guide, Kit Carson, back in the 1840s.

Tahosa Valley, which runs north to south along the eastern slope of Longs Peak, was almost called Elkanah Valley, after the mountaineering minister mentioned earlier. But the Colorado Geographic Board selected *Tahosa*, the Kiowa Indian word for "the top of the mountains." Incidentally, had the U. S. Congress reconsidered before admitting Colorado into the Union, it might have been called Tahosa instead of Colorado.

Teddy's Teeth, a series of rock outcroppings, is on the side of Rams Horn Mountain. Political cartoonists during Theodore Roosevelt's presidency relished in exaggerating the quantity and size of his teeth for humorous effect. The name of these outcroppings derives from these exaggerations. Let us hope that other groups of conspicuous rock formations will not be burdened with modern variations on that theme. "Jimmy's Teeth" just doesn't have the same ring to it.

The names of many other park features honor people prominent in local history: Lambs Slide on Longs Peak, named for Elkanah Lamb's harrowing East Face descent; Mills Lake, for Enos Mills; Mount Dickinson for the first woman to climb Longs Peak; Mount Dunraven, for the famous "Earl of Estes Park"; and Jims Grove on the Longs Peak trail, for Rocky Mountain Jim.

The place-names on topographical maps for this region reflect the colorful history of the area. The spectrum of people who have inhabited this area has ranged from nomadic Arapaho to nomadic modern-day tourists; from a Kansas farm boy who eventually helped establish a national park to an aristocratic Englishman who was unable to establish a personal park. The testaments to the history of this area are indelibly written in the valleys, mountains, and lakes of Rocky Mountain National Park.

Chapter 2

Natural History

GEOLOGY

Geology also gives us important clues to the history of Rocky Mountain National Park. Massive upheavals, volcanic action, and glacial scarring created the mountains and valleys of the park. To read this history, the student must study the earth itself.

Rocks are divided into three classes: *sedimentary*, those deposited by wind, water, or ice; *igneous*, those cooled from a molten state; and *metamorphic*, those that were formed from the other two by heat and pressure. The rock beneath the park was formed 1.8 billion years ago. This ancient rock is of two types: gneiss (pronounced "nice") and schist. Both are composed of the minerals feldspar, quarts, and mica. Though they differ slightly in the crystal arrangement of their components, both are noticeably banded or streaked. These metamorphic rocks developed from clay, silt, and sand from ancient lakes and oceans. As these materials were covered by additional deposits over eons, they underwent staggering amounts of pressure and heat, forming harder rocks, with new materials.

Granite, an element common to many of the mountains in the region, is a younger rock, formed as molten rock (magma) was forced up into the schist and gneiss layers. This massive intrusion of magma into the contorted and twisted layers of older rock occurred several times over a period of millions of years. Granite consists of essentially the same minerals as the older gneiss and schist, but has larger and better defined crystals. Pegmatite, which later intruded into the masses of granite, and contains the same material, is conspicuous for even larger crystals.

THE BIRTH OF THE ROCKIES

The Rockies began to be formed almost 530 million years ago. At that time, this entire region was covered with water—one of many seas that encroached on and later receded from this area. But approximately 300 million years ago, a massive upheaval from the depths of the earth's crust gradually raised the rock above the water. But even as these early mountains, the Ancestral Rockies, rose, they were eroded by water. Sixty million years of this inexorable process reduced the Ancestral Rockies to low, gentle hills. The sea, which had been biding its time, began returning to its former home. As the sea began to cover the land, it was preceded by great sand dunes. The sea remained in this area for 50 million years, and deposited enormous amounts of sand and sediments.

THE SECOND ROCKY MOUNTAINS

Eventually, 190 million years ago, renewed uplift from the earth's crust caused the sea to retreat as before. This time, it left thousands of feet of sandstone and other sedimentary rock, formed by the compaction of sand and silt debris over 50 million years. The *sandstone hogbacks*, the elongated ridges just east of the foothills, are the result of this deposit of sediment.

The uplift that drove away the water was relatively minor, and, once a sufficient quantity of land had been eroded and carried off by rivers, the sea returned. This time the sea remained for 30 million years, redepositing sand and silt. As this debris was deposited on the floor of the sea, the intense pressure of the water formed it into sandstone and shale.

Seventy million years ago uplift again caused the water to retreat. This time the sea had left almost 5,000 feet of sedimentary rock as a top layer or cap over the metamorphic rock deep below. But once again, sandstone and shale were eroded, eliminating much of it within the relatively short span of 3 million years. But this sedimentary rock was not entirely washed away. Today, deposits of shale containing fossils from this period can be seen in the northern part of the Never Summer Mountains. The mountains exposed after the sedimentary cap was eroded were composed of ancient gneiss and shist. The elevation of these Second Rocky Mountains was probably no more than 2,500 feet above the surrounding plains, and no more than 3,000 feet above sea level.

Volcanic activity began 54 million years ago in these decaying mountains, near the present-day site of Mount Richthofen in the Never Summers. There is evidence of this ancient volcano in the congealed volcanic deposits on Richthofen's eastern and southern slopes. The end of the Second Rocky Mountains came approximately 40 million years ago, when they were once again reduced to rolling hills.

THE PRESENT ROCKIES

The first of several more uplifts began 40 million years ago, and brought the mountains up to a height of 6,000 feet. But unlike earlier uplifts, this one brought on massive volcanic activity. Between 37 and 34 million years ago, volcanoes south and west of the peak's current location spewed trillions of tons of ash and debris into the air. Carried by winds, the ash fell in mountainous quantities in the area that later became the park. The ash filled whole valleys, almost covering the smaller mountains to the east and west.

Uneven uplift created gigantic fractures, contributing to the volcanic activity that occurred 28 million years ago in the vicinity of Lulu Mountain. Ash flow rock, created by the collapse of thick deposits of hot ash, lava flows, airborne volcanic debris, obsidian, and mudflows, spread out over a large region. The old deposits on Mount Richthofen became covered with this new ash flow, and the deep canyons where Milner and La Poudre passes are today were filled. The results of this incredible volcanic activity can be seen at Iceberg Lake on Trail Ridge Road. The head wall to the west is solid volcanic debris, the remnants of a valley that was filled to a depth of five hundred feet.

Specimen Mountain has long been regarded as the source of this and other volcanic deposits in the area. But new geologic studies indicate that at the time of these tremendous deposits of debris, it could not have been an active volcano. The reason is that it too is covered with ash flow, originating from a point to the northwest. The Iceberg Lake and Specimen Mountain deposits are quite possibly from the same source.

Eighteen million years ago, uplift, which had been somewhat inactive for millions of years, resumed, as did erosion at an accelerated pace. Much of the volcanic debris was swept away, and deposited and *lithified* elsewhere.* The enormous quantity of volcanic sediment washed away during this period literally covered the mountains to the north in Wyoming. Valleys in the park that had become filled became retrenched by the powerful force of moving water. The uplift brought the Rockies to an elevation about 4,000 feet below what they are today.

The final uplift, which occurred 5 to 7 million years ago, raised the mountains another 4,000 to 5,000 feet. Typical of its previous growth, the uplift was uneven, causing great fracturing and faulting. This time the faulting did not cause the staggering vulcanism of previous times. Had it done so, Rocky Mountain National Park would be a far different place today. Not only did this final uplift eliminate the volcanic debris, it was also a time of great erosion. Rivers began flowing through fractures in the crust, forming new valleys. The stage was then set for a new force to enter into the complex history of the formation of Rocky Mountain National Park. About 2 million years ago (a brief flash of time in geologic history) the world climate began changing, and the advent of glaciers was at hand.

GLACIERS, THE SCULPTORS OF THE ROCKIES

The last 2 million years of earth history is called the Quaternary era or, more popularly, the Ice Age. It has been characterized by alternating cold and warm periods, each lasting thousands of years. It is not known how many fluctu-

**Lithified* means petrified or turned to stone.

ations there have been during this era. But with the change to colder climate, huge expanses of ice formed, changing the face of the land. When the Ice Age began, the valleys of Rocky Mountain National Park were typical of those cut by water: *V*-shaped, with steep sides and a narrow channel at the bottom. Glaciers formed from the first snowfall along the continental divide, filling, at first, the small crevices between rocks, and then spreading to the tops of the steep canyons. As snow fell and temperatures decreased the snow got increasingly deeper. Over the relatively short period of twenty to thirty years, the snow compacted into solid ice. The masses of ice forming at the top of the steep valleys moved downslope when their weight reached a critical point. As they moved, they were fed by repeated snowfalls.

Glaciers chipped away rock at the tops and sides of valleys. Ice formed in the cracks, expanding them further. Eventually the rock broke away, and was transported down with the glacier. This debris, as well as the enormous quantity of debris pushed along by the glacier, formed elongated ridges and debris piles, called *moraines.* There are dozens of moraines throughout the park. Examination of moraines tells geologists about the chronology and extent of glacial activity in the area. Composition, shape, directional alignment, and height all offer clues to the past.

It is easy to see how a huge glacier could gouge out rock and widen a whole valley. That is why a *U*-shaped valley is evidence of one carved by a glacier, while a *V*-shaped one is the result of water or faulting. For a good example of glaciation, stand in Moraine Park looking west. There lateral moraines flank a *U*-shaped valley.

In the park, you can find glacial evidence of an ice age 160,000 years ago. This period, known as the *intermediate glaciation*, was preceded by early glacial and interglacial periods, though there is no physical evidence of the latter two locally. An earlier intermediate glacial period, called Bull Lake glaciation, extended from 127,000 to 87,000 years ago. Large rivers of ice, originating at the top of present-day canyons, flowed into the valleys, filling them to a depth of 2,000 feet, and extending to points outside the present park boundaries. Many moraines from this glaciation are evident in the park today. Another period of glaciation in the park area began after a warm interlude about 70,000 years ago. The ice returned in the form of glaciers 45,000 years ago, and receded 13,000 years later.

The last widespread glaciation began about 27,000 years ago, after another warm interlude. These glaciers probably peaked in size 12,000 years later, when ice, 1,500 feet thick, flowed in frozen rivers eight to ten miles long down every major canyon in the park. The largest glacier in the park region originated at La Poudre Pass in the northern Never Summers, and flowed south to Shadow Mountain Reservoir, twenty miles away. This last period of glaciation put the finishing touches on places such as the east face of Longs Peak. The canyons, cirques, and rock faces were carved and slashed by the activity of the ice.

Thirty-eight hundred years ago a minor period of cooling brought back the glaciers. This period is called the Little Ice Age or *neoglaciation.* A cooling between 100 A.D. and 1000 A.D., and another during the last 300 years, created larger glaciers than are seen today.

The effect of glaciation has been to enlarge and deepen the canyons of the park. By driving on Trail Ridge Road or hiking along the continental divide, you can see graphic evidence of the work of ice. The relatively flat tundra adjacent to steep gorges was formed by continuous repetitions of freezing and thawing. This flat tundra expanse, called the flattop peneplain, is what is left of the high rounded mountain tops of the last great uplift. Ice has eroded the head walls of the valleys of this high plain, much like water does when running down a dirt embankment. If there were another period of cooling and ice formation, erosion by ice would eat away further at the rolling alpine expanses, such as Big Horn Flats and the Trail Ridge Road tundra.

It may come as a disappointment to learn that the glaciers in Rocky Mountain National Park are no longer rivers of ice like the glaciers of Mount McKinley or Mount Rainier. The glaciers here are reduced by factors of average temperature and snowline to mere remnants of their former size. The principal glaciers today are: Tyndall Glacier, between Hallett Peak and Flattop Mountain; Rowe Glacier, north of Hagues Peak; Andrews Glacier, in the Loch; and Taylor Glacier, also in The Loch above Sky Pond. Less prominent glaciers include Spragues Glacier, near Stones Peak; Moomaw Glacier, north of Isolation Peak in Wild Basin; Mills Glacier, on the east face of Longs Peak; and Chiefs Head Glacier, in upper Glacier Gorge.

This discussion of the geology of the park has focussed on events from 1.8 billion years ago to those of the last 300 years, quite a span of time. But though we analyze it as history, the same geological forces and climate fluctuations still persist. Six thousand years from now there may be new glaciers in the mountains of this area. Ten million years from now, volcanoes may once again spew hot ash and deadly gases into the air. We are here for such a brief time that it is difficult to fully grasp the enormous amount of time it has taken to form the rock of these mountains. The forces that have worked on these peaks and valleys will continue in the same way for eons.

FLORA

We have seen that the glacial history of the park is closely tied to climatic variations. When the average annual temperature dropped for long periods, glaciers formed, changing the face of the land. Plant life in Rocky Mountain National Park has a similar relation to environmental factors. Certain types of plants today are dominant at specific elevations because of their suitability to existing factors of temperature, moisture, and soil composition. The dominance of any plant group is dependent to a large extent on climate.

When the last period of widespread glaciation took place, much of the park was as barren as the highest point on Trail Ridge Road today. Trees, shrubs, flowers, and ferns did not flourish as they now do. But as the ice retreated, the plant communities advanced. The arctic vegetation was gradually superseded by the vegetation common today.

The barren, glacier-scarred rock was first taken over by lichens, the platelike growths of fungus and algae seen growing on rocks. These lichens established soil by combining minerals and decaying vegetable matter. Once a primitive soil was established, other forms of plants could grow and contribute to still more soil. Eventually, a complex system of plant life developed, creating meadows, forests, and the deceptively barren expanses of tundra we presently see.

There are three basic zones of plant growth in the park, each associated with specific elevations. The lowest, the Montane zone, ranges from approximately 6,000 to 9,000 feet above sea level. The Subalpine zone is from 9,000 to roughly 11,500 feet. Above elevations of 10,500 to 11,500 feet is the Alpine zone.

Let's begin with the lower elevations, and work up toward the tops of the mountains. This is similar to traveling north toward the Arctic Circle, since that area compares to that above 11,500 feet in north-central Colorado. The further north you go, the lower this zone will be. For instance, timberline, which heralds the Alpine zone, is at about 9,000 feet in Montana and near 7,000 feet in Alberta, Canada. The Montane zone is sometimes called the Canadian zone for its similarity to the environment of Canadian latitudes. The Subalpine zone is called Hudsonian for its resemblance to the Hudson Bay country of northern Canada.

THE MONTANE ZONE

In those areas of the park below 9,000 feet, the climate is relatively warm and dry. The vegetation typically includes scattered forested areas, intermingled with open meadows. The area around the national park headquarters is a good example of this. It is here that the ponderosa pine is most common. The bark of the ponderosa, a kind of conifer or cone-bearing tree, consists of reddish-brown plates. It has dull green needles, varying from three to six inches in length, longer than any of the other pines in the park. The needles appear on the branches in distinguishable clusters. Over the past several years, this hearty tree has been attacked by a deadly pine beetle. Unfortunately, huge stands have been decimated all along the front range of the Rockies, where it has spawned the nickname of "Colorado golden pine" because of the dried-out, dead needles. The ponderosa thrives on the warmer, south-facing slopes, which receive the greatest amount of solar radiation year round.

The cooler and wetter north slopes also support ponderosa, but are favored by the Douglas fir. The easiest way to spot this tree is by its needles, which are usually about one inch long and flat, with a sort of stalk at the bottom. Also, they grow singly along the branch rather than in clusters. The bark is a smooth gray in young trees, becoming brownish and rough in the older ones. Its cones average two inches in length, and have wide scales, with three-pronged tufts or *bracts* emanating from them.

Another conifer common to the park is the beautiful blue spruce. This tree frequents wetter locations, near lakes or along watercourses. It resembles the firs, but its cones are longer, three to five inches, and lack the bracts found on the Douglas fir. Its name derives from the distinctive silver-bluish hue of the needles.

The lodgepole pine normally grows in the higher elevations of the Montane and into the Subalpine zone. Its name derives from its use as the framework for the tipis or lodges of the American plains Indians. It grows straight, has thin bark, and has a slender trunk, rarely exceeding twenty inches in circumference. Cones, usually about two inches long, in clusters of two or three, are tightly attached to the branches, and often remain intact many years. Since lodgepole cones open after exposure to forest fires, dense stands of these trees frequently signify past fires.

The juniper, or more properly, Rocky Mountain juniper, also grows in the Montane zone. It is not a cone-bearing tree, and it technically has no needles. Instead, this juniper has small, branched, flattened leaves, which bear bright blue berries. It is not a tall, slender tree, but rather more of a large shrub. It favors the drier climates of the park, and is common to rocky, south-facing slopes.

Of the *deciduous* trees in the park, the best known is unquestionably the quaking aspen, or simply, aspen.* The name

*Deciduous trees shed their leaves seasonally, or at a certain stage of development.

quaking refers to the way the leaves flutter in even the slightest breeze. In the fall, the aspen trees in the park are as much of a tourist attraction as the mountains themselves. The golden color of the aspen leaves in autumn, highlighted by the dark green forests surrounding them, is a magnificent sight. They are immediately identifiable as deciduous trees, and have a smooth, white bark, dotted with black. Their leaves are a soft green color and have a distinctive upside-down heart shape. They grow well into the Subalpine zone, as do many of the trees of this lower zone, and are more inclined to grow on south-facing slopes. The various other deciduous trees in the park grow most abundantly in the Montane zone. Among them are water birch, thinleaf alder, narrowleaf cottonwood, and Rocky Mountain maple.

Regrettably, it is impossible in the short space permitted to detail the flowers of Rocky Mountain National Park. Even the discussion of the principal trees, although much fewer in number, is necessarily brief. Two particularly good books listed in the Bibliography go into the subject extensively, and the reader with an interest in flowers is urged to investigate them.

THE SUBALPINE ZONE

Above 9,000 feet in elevation, the forest changes character. The scattered groves of trees and the numerous meadows give way to the more dense, expansive stands of timber characterizing the Subalpine zone. Although this zone sustains several species of trees found in the Montane zone, it also has some inhabitants characteristic of higher elevations.

The Englemann spruce is one of the most typical species of this zone. These trees grow straight and tall in the crisp, high-altitude air, tapering upward to a point. The branches are almost horizontal, and droop slightly. Its four-sided needles are in compact arrangements, encircling the twigs to which they cling. The cones display individual platelets, which are notched, toothed, or pointed at the tips. The Englemann spruce and its common neighbor, subalpine fir, both benefit from increased moisture, in the form of rain and snow, found at this altitude.

The subalpine fir is distinct from its relative, the Douglas fir, in that its cones are fewer in number, located more toward the top of the tree, and lack the typical three-branched bracts. Though this fir resembles the Englemann spruce, the flat, dull-tipped needles distinguish it from the four-sided sharper needles of the Englemann.

The vast spruce-fir forests of the park are said to be *climax forests*. This means that a number of species have inhabited these forests, to the point where no other species will intrude and become dominant. As an example, let's suppose a huge forest is decimated by a forest fire. After various plants and shrubs flourish, the first tree to gain a foothold is usually the aspen. Slowly, lodgepole pine enter and gain dominance, eventually driving out the aspen. After many more years, lodgepole forests are invaded by spruce and fir, which cohabitate well. Spruce and fir establish dominance, and the lodgepole goes the way of its predecessors. Since no other species challenge their position of dominance, they become the climax growth of this zone.

The upper subalpine or Hudsonian zone, 10,500 to 11,500 feet, is usually sparsely timbered. Those that grow here are often the limber pine, characterized by gnarled, twisted growth, a product of the often savage environment at this altitude. Their branches usually grow only on the opposite side of the tree from the prevailing wind, which in winter is almost ceaseless. They adapt, though, and sometimes grow in bizarre clumps, close to the ground, behind a cover of rocks, resembling dense evergreen shrubs. Cones are often six inches long, longer than any other conifer in Colorado.

THE ALPINE ZONE

This treeless expanse of tundra covers almost one quarter of Rocky Mountain National Park. The average daytime high temperature during the summer months is 50° F. At this altitude, it can snow any day of the year, and there is vegetation to stop the wind when it blows furiously—sometimes seventy-five mph. At first glance tundra appears barren, but that is deceiving. The cushionlike, spongy tundra grass is intertwined with an awesome array of alpine flowers: alpine buttercup, bright blue alpine forget-me-not, fairy primrose, mountain dryad, and dozens of others. Lichens, the first plants to invade the rock after the glaciers retreated, are also evident here. Though such frail-looking flowers seem out of place in an environment with such potential for hostility, they survive well. But man can wreck havoc where nature does not. Tundra is in extremely delicate balance, and it takes many years for regrowth to cover the scars of overuse. Areas of the tundra have growing seasons counted in days, or at most, weeks. It is important to approach this fragile area with care.

If you have an opportunity, visit the Alpine Visitor Center on Trail Ridge Road for a first-hand examination of this alpine environment. They have an excellent natural history display there, as well as rangers to answer your questions.

FAUNA

We will now take a look at the principal animals of Rocky Mountain National Park—those the visitor is most likely to see, and a few less common.

HOOFED ANIMALS

The Algonquian Indian name for the elk was *Wapiti.* This animal is larger than a deer, with a more brownish or even reddish coat. Its antlers have a wider spread than its smaller relatives, the deer, and are greater in size. Elk were originally found predominantly on the plains and lower foothills. Man's intrusion has driven them to the high-country, where they are found today during the warmer months. With the snows of autumn, they descend to the lower meadows. In September and October, Horseshoe Park is a good place to catch a glimpse of the herds feeding at sunset. Autumn is also the mating season, and the bugling of the bull elk is evidence of their open challenges to each other for dominance.

These magnificent creatures were almost exterminated in the park region by decades of hunting. But in 1914, just prior to the formation of the park, many elk were transplanted here from Yellowstone National Park to keep the elk a viable species in this area. This venture was partially funded by the eccentric inventor and hotel operator, F. O. Stanley. The elk

Mule deer. This is a mature male with large, well-developed antlers. These animals are common in the park. (Photograph courtesy of the National Park Service.)

thrive today because hunting is prohibited within the park's boundaries. In addition, the age-old enemies of the elk—mountain lion, wolf, and grizzly bear—have either been driven away or greatly reduced in number.

Mule deer share the range with the elk, but are more prevalent and more visible to park visitors. They do not grow as big as elk, although some attain impressive size. The males of both mule deer and elk have antlers. During late winter and early spring they are without these defensive weapons, but as summer approaches antlers develop, and until late-August bear a soft, fuzzy covering called *velvet.* This velvet comes off when the silent signal of instinct causes the elk and deer to rub their antlers on trees. Shortly, antlers become polished, beautiful horns. It is unusual to find a full, undamaged set of antlers in the wild after they are shed. Since antlers contain calcium and salt, various rodents and porcupines find them a great delicacy.

Bighorn sheep are also famous park residents. Like the elk, the bighorns were threatened with extinction locally. But

The Rocky Mountain bighorn sheep. These magnificent animals were almost extinct in the park area sixty years ago. But protection within the park's boundaries has helped bring them back in encouraging numbers. (Photograph by Robert Waltermire.)

protection against hunters has helped save the elk and bighorns, also known as mountain sheep. The principal range for the bighorn within the park is the area of Specimen Mountain and north. Throughout the years, bighorns have appeared in Horseshoe Park at the appropriately named Sheep Lakes. They are also seen in the northern Never Summers and outside the park boundary toward Poudre Canyon. During their early winter mating season, when the mature rams fight for dominance over the females, the clash of rams' horns sounds like rifle fire. If you intend to photograph any bighorn sheep, you will probably need a telephoto lens. They are extremely leery of intruders into their mountain home, and flee quickly. The hunters' guns have been still in Rocky Mountain National Park for over sixty years. But I suspect the bighorn sheep have a collective consciousness that has not forgotten.

THE PREDATORS

The large predators of the past are all but gone in Rocky Mountain National Park. Of the grizzly bear, black bear, mountain lion, and timber wolf, only a very few black bear and mountain lion (also called cougar) remain. The black bears are very difficult to spot because of their reduced numbers. They have not degenerated into beggars, as in Yellowstone, and stay away from civilization as much as possible. Every now and again, though, they supplement their diet of berries, ants, frogs, roots, carrion, and mice with a multi-course meal of garbage near the campgrounds, guest ranches, and homes on both sides of the park.

Mountain lions are an extremely rare sight, even in places outside the park, where they exist in greater numbers. In the wild, they can see, hear, and smell humans long before there is any chance of being discovered. The myth that crafty, blood-thirsty cougars crouch regularly on limbs and rock outcroppings, overhanging well-used trails is absurd.

Coyotes, which are more often heard than seen, have a high-pitched, staccato yelp. Their calls, occasionally heard while sitting around an evening campfire, add an intriguing touch to the camping experience.

The red fox, a smaller relative of the coyote, can also be found in the park. They are smaller than their much-maligned cousins, and are rightfully known for their cunning. Both these animals generally feed on small rodents.

The bobcat is a beautiful creature, almost as rare to spot as the mountain lion. The author has seen only one—on the Storm Pass trail near Estes Cone. They feed on small rodents, rabbits, and birds, and are patient, skilled hunters.

The mink, marten, and weasel are related, both genetically and in their habits. All are voracious eaters. The mink tends to stay near water, and feeds principally on frogs, fish, and small rodents. The weasel is more adapted to woodlands, and will attack and kill almost any rodent it can find. Weasels turn pure white in the winter, except for the very tip of their tails, which remains black. Martens are at home on the forest floor or in treetops. They hunt squirrels and birds, which may be complacent in the false security of high branches. Like the weasels and mink, martens also feed on fish, rodents of every description, frogs, and insects. The author awoke one evening at Thunder Lake to see a large mar-

The Marmot. This large rodent is quite prevalent in the park. (Photograph by the author.)

ten hauling off a heavy stuff-sack filled with food. It seems their diet also includes canned mandarin oranges, swiss cheese, and freeze-dried turkey tetrazzini.

RODENTS AND RABBITS

Since there are many species of rodents and rabbits in the park, we will look at a few of the more important ones you are likely to see. The beaver, which was trapped almost to extinction, is abundant in the park. A description of the dams and lodges they build is unnecessary, for almost everyone is acquainted with the habits of these industrious creatures. All over the park, the chisled stumps of deciduous trees, particularly aspen, attest to their presence. Since they work and play at night, dusk is a good time to spot them. Some beavers attain incredible size, weighing as much as ninety pounds.

The smaller relative of the beaver is the muskrat, which lives in or near water, but does not build dams. They do build lodges, but on a smaller scale. Some muskrats burrow into stream banks and build homes in subterranean chambers. While the beaver is strictly vegetarian, the muskrat will eat insects and fish. In appearance, the two animals are similar; the major difference is the flat tail of the beaver versus the slender tail of the smaller muskrat.

The marmot is a clumsy looking, grizzly-gray rodent, which is a bit smaller than a beaver. Marmots are common all over the park, but are more conspicuous at higher altitudes.

Conys or pikas are interesting rodents, found scampering among the rock-strewn areas at timberline. They look like fat, grey ground squirrels with noticeably rounded ears. They are vociferous creatures, whose calls are reminiscent of the high-pitched chirps of birds.

Snowshoe rabbits are aptly named. Their hind feet are absurdly large in order to support the weight of their bodies while traveling in the snow. Like the weasel, one of their natural enemies, they turn white in winter.

Chipmunks and ground squirrels are found everywhere in the park. Virtually any wide spot on Trail Ridge Road, substantial enough for a parked car, will be visited by these rodents, waiting for a handout.

BIRDS

Several varieties of birds live in the park. One of the most common, at least as far as campers are concerned, is the Rocky Mountain jay, known as the "camp robber." These birds willingly swoop down to eat morsels held in the hand, and have been known to eat part of your dinner if you aren't looking. The Clark's nutcracker, which resembles the jay, is called a "camp robber" for the same reason. The best way to distinguish between the two birds is the length of the beak. The beak of the Clark's nutcracker is more elongated and slender.

Magpies are noisy black and white birds, commonly found feeding on carrion along highways and roads. They have characteristically long tail-feathers. Magpies are scavengers, and may also be "camp robbers" when the opportunity presents itself.

The ptarmigan (silent *p*) is an alpine grouse, whose camouflage is so excellent that it can be difficult to see them from as close as ten feet. In winter, their plumage changes to white, so they blend in with a winter environment as well. And well they should: many predators find ptarmigan a delicacy.

While both eagles and hawks are found in the park, the latter is much more prevalent. Of the hawks found here, the redwing hawk is one of the most common. Golden eagles, whose tail-feathers have been traditionally coveted by American Indians, are rarely seen in the park. Even rarer is the bald eagle, our national symbol, which may become extinct some horrible day. If you spot a large bird soaring on thermal currents, it is most likely a hawk. If the bird is not too high, a good way to distinguish between a hawk and an eagle is to study the wings. The wings of eagles are normally wider and more rounded at the tips than that of hawks. The eagles' wings also appear straighter in flight, with only a slight angle visible where the tip feathers meet the wing. If you do see an eagle in the wild within the park, savor the experience, for it unfortunately comes only to a few. These birds, appropriate symbols of untamed freedom, can uplift the spirit unlike few other sights.

Part Two

Preparation for the Trail

Chapter 3

Equipment

Many backpackers who come to the park are already prepared with camping and hiking paraphernalia. This discussion on equipment is intended for both novice campers and those in the process of improving their camping gear. Fluctuations in prices preclude listing current costs, though this is admittedly an important criteria for equipment selection. Current prices can be obtained at the mountaineering shops in Estes Park, Grand Lake, and elsewhere.

BOOTS

Good-fitting footwear is more critical to the enjoyment of hiking than almost any other factor. As with all camping equipment, it makes good sense to buy quality products. Specialty mountaineering stores are the best places to obtain hiking boots. Employees of these shops are usually hikers themselves, and their experience with boot fit can be invaluable.

You should have a reasonably good idea of how the boot will be used before making a purchase. A serious mountaineer, who will use boots on long trips over rough terrain, should consider a boot with at least a three-quarter length steel shank. The shank is built into the inner sole for reinforcement. Klettershues, which are lighter, more flexible boots, are suitable for light hiking. Full-grain leather (with a naturally water-resistant layer of hide) is very important to the life span of the boot. Durable, full-grain leather waterproofs much more efficiently, and consequently resists warping and excessive drying.

Two socks, a light inner and a heavy outer, ought to be worn when hiking. The heavier outer sock (frequently composed of wool) offers padding and insulation in cooler weather. The inner sock (which should wick moisture away from the foot) should fit snugly to cut down friction and reduce the probability of blisters. Finally, don't expect to walk out of the backpacking shop and begin your continental divide traverse. Even with a good fit, it takes time before the boot begins to conform to the foot and the foot toughens and adapts to the boot.

PACKS

As with boots, fit is the most important criteria for choosing a pack. Similarly, before buying, one should establish how the pack will be used. The trail hiker who hasn't any interest in overnight trips should consider a light, well-made rucksack. Its size should correspond to the amount the individual will carry. A simple collection, including lunch, a water bottle, a camera, and a Windbreaker doesn't require much volume. But then add extra camera lenses, a wool sweater, a pack rod and tackle, a rain poncho, toilet paper, maps, and a first-aid kit. In short, try to establish how much volume you will require for the type of hiking you will do.

There are two basic types of packs on the market today, internal and external frame design. The external frame pack is the conventional style with the pack material attached to an aluminum or aluminum alloy pack frame. The internal frame looks like a large rucksack with no apparent support. But the frame is built-in, usually with flat aluminum slats for support. The advantage of this pack is balance, since the closer it rides to the back, the better it will feel. The external frame, however, is cooler to wear because of the space between the padded frame and your back. This, the more conventional of the two, is recommended for the beginner.

Framed packs are usually used for backpacking on overnight trips. The same size considerations apply here as well. But fit becomes more important, since longer trips require more equipment and hence more weight to distribute comfortably. When shopping for a frame pack, try on several models. Even a poorly fitting pack feels alright unweighted. One good way to put weight on a pack is to have someone stand behind you, and pull down on both sides of the pack. Better yet, place twenty or thirty pounds of sandbags or other weights inside the pack. Shift these weights within the pack to feel how this affects the center of gravity.

Most frame packs are now equipped with padded hip belts as well as padded shoulder straps. There are as many theories on how and where to carry the load as there are styles of packs. But it can be said that by packing the heavier items close to the back and behind the shoulders, the center of gravity of the load will be primarily over the hips and spine. Tightening the hip belt and moving the pack slightly up will center the weight around the hips, while loosening the hip belt will shift more weight back to the shoulders. After hiking a short distance, you can establish where the weight feels best. Specialty-shop assistance will again be helpful here. Remember to choose a pack as you would a pair of boots—for fit, not appearance.

TENTS

Choosing the right backpacking tent for your needs is a bit more difficult than selecting boots or a pack. You don't wear your tent; but you will live in it. Consequently, let us begin by discussing size as a criteria for selection. Normally a two-person tent is sufficient. Most two-person tents can accommodate two large people plus some equipment. Winter mountaineering tents are generally large enough to hold two people and all their equipment. Packs and excess gear can be left outside the tent during spring, summer, and fall. If you get "cabin fever" easily in a two-person tent and wish to carry a three- or four-person tent, just remember that out on the trail your desire for more space may be replaced with a profound affection for lighter, smaller tents. If there is one four-person tent for a party of four, distribute the weight evenly among each hiker. One can carry the tent only, while the others carry the stakes, tent poles, and rain fly.

Condensation of moisture within the tent can be a problem. This is the principal reason most good quality mountaineering tents have breathable tops or canopies. The moisture from perspiration and breath can pass through the nylon to the outside. The waterproof rain fly, not the tent canopy, is what keeps the rain from entering. The backpacker is advised to rent or purchase a tent with these features. Lack of foresight may mean waking in the morning to the stark realization of just how much moisture can collect on the inside of an enclosed waterproof shelter. It is most uncomfortable to sleep in a tent, when its floor bears a disconcerting similarity to the Everglades.

Even with a tent that "breathes," it's a good idea to have it ventilated at both ends. Frequently tents include a rear "window" of sorts that is mosquito-netted and has a zippered flap to close it off during inclement weather.

The snow tunnels found on some tents are, for obvious reasons, a waste of money for the summer camper. But since they can be invaluable for winter camping, it is a feature to keep in mind if you plan to camp in January as well as June. Not only are two entrances convenient, but the improved cross-ventilation helps reduce condensation.

Most two-person nylon tents made today are in the six- to eight-pound range. But extremely lightweight, inexpensive shelters known as tube tents can be purchased. Essentially, the tube tent is an item you carry on an overnight, but hope you won't have to use. It is a plastic tube, usually about ten feet long. Folded up, it is very compact. To erect a tube tent, when that rainstorm you were hoping wouldn't materialize begins to threaten, you string a piece of cord from a tree through the tube tent to another tree. Open up the ends and place inside equipment, stones, or small logs to expand the bottom widthwise. The result is an elongated triangular piece of plastic open at both ends. It will keep you dry in a moderate rain, but don't expect miracles in any kind of wind.

If you are shopping for a mountaineering tent you have many brands from which to choose. But you will have to choose between two basic tent styles–dome-shaped or the traditional peaked-roof design. The latter is referred to as an

A-frame if the tent poles are enclosed in sleeves on both sides of the tent's forward and rear ends. The reason for this method of construction is that it is stronger in high winds and is generally more stable.

The dome tents seen on the market recently are excellent tents, but usually more expensive. Their advantage is space. Even with the two-person models, they are roomier than their A-frame counterparts. Assuming equivalent quality, the dome tents are just as strong as any A-frame, but usually heavier.

Regardless of what kind of tent you choose, select a location away from low-lying areas, and set up the tent with the "door" away from the wind. Camping right next to a river or lake has a special charm for some. But since the ground and air may be damp near rivers and lakes, this can be uncomfortable. Sometimes it's difficult to pry oneself out of that cozy sleeping bag when it's chilly and dark in the tent. So try to visualize where the sun will shine in the early morning hours and set up camp there.

With increased visitor use in almost all backpacking areas in Rocky Mountain National Park, it would be good to mention some personal thoughts on tent colors. Even though the camper knows, when he is on the trail, that there may be thousands of other such enthusiasts in the park, it is, quite frankly, more pleasant to feel as divorced from civilization as possible. It is difficult to feel that you're really away from it all, when you can look down across a valley and see little orange dots. The national parks are a place to blend in, not stand out. More tent manufacturers are recognizing this change in attitude. While international orange may be good for winter situations where visibility is desirable as a safety precaution, it is not justifiable for summer camping. If you need a bright-colored tent to find your way back to camp, it would be best to invest in a map and compass. Additionally, some campers and entymologists have suggested that bright colors attract flies and other insects more readily than earth tones and subtle shades. Having now alienated readers who own orange tents, we will proceed, with no hard feelings, to sleeping bags.

SLEEPING BAGS

There are presently two predominant types of sleeping bags available on the market: those made of goose or duck down and the relatively new synthetic fills such as Polarguard and Fiberfill. The differences between the synthetics are so minor that they do not warrant mention here.

Synthetic sleeping bags have come a long way in the last few years in quality and insulating efficiency. Far superior to the old cotton- or dacron-filled bags, these new synthetics are now giving traditional down bags some pretty fair competition in the marketplace. The principal advantage of synthetics is cost. One might spend 50 percent less for a synthetic bag rated to approximately 15°-20° F than for a down bag of comparable quality and comfort. Another advantage is the synthetic's ability to retain its loft, and therefore its insulating properties, when wet. (Remember that watertight tent whose floor resembled the Everglades in the morning?) If you camp out in the open and there is a heavy dew, the synthetic will dry readily when hung on a tree limb for about an hour.

Down sleeping bags, however, remain the most popular (though this statement could become outdated soon). Although they lose loft when damp and are more expensive than synthetic bags, traditional goose down is about the most efficient insulator for its weight that you can buy. While synthetic bags may need three pounds of fill to insulate to 15° F, the down bag will only require about two pounds. In addition, down compacts more easily and tighter than synthetics, when put into a stuff sack for hiking. Where space and weight are important considerations, the down bag is the one to consider.

Virtually all backpacking sleeping bags are now made with two-way nylon zippers, either tooth or coil type. Nylon zippers are easier to operate than metal zippers, and their ability to zip from the top or the bottom allows the user to ventilate the bag during the night. This is a real advantage if you own a bag rated to 0° F, and the low temperature at night will be 50° F. Leaving the bottom part unzipped a bit allows excessive heat from inside to escape. After a few nights on the trail, the right position for the zipper can be found. The two-way zippers also allow two bags with corresponding zipper sides and size to be connected into one large bag. The advantage of this option is best left to each individual to contemplate.

But even a warm, good quality sleeping bag can be cold and uncomfortable without a sleeping pad. Sleeping pads are usually made from either open- or closed-cell foam. The open cell, similar to foam rubber, is generally enclosed in a waterproof nylon covering. As it is soft to lie on, its advantage is comfort. But closed-cell foam is a better insulator. Because each tiny air pocket within the pad is sealed, there is no movement of air. "Dead air," as it is called, is one of the best insulators. Another reason closed-cell pads are superior is that they do not absorb moisture. Most popular among the closed-cell pads is a product called Ensolite. In addition to their other advantages, Ensolite pads are less expensive than open-cell pads, and roll up tighter for packing. Air mattresses are favored by some, but even a small leak will cause air movement beneath you during the night. This will draw warmth from the sleeping bag. If the leak is big enough, it won't be long before you'll be sleeping right on the ground.

COOKING PARAPHERNALIA

Among the conservation practices advocated by the national parks in recent years is the emphasis on using camp stoves instead of campfires for cooking. There are several reasons for this. Campfires require foraging for wood and may result in live wood being torn and cut from trees. Not only is this inexcusable from a conservationist's standpoint, but it does not take much camping experience to know that dead wood burns better than "green" wood. Campfires, when confined to designated fire pits in those park campsites where permitted, are not as much of an eyesore. But when a camper encounters an area where fire rings of charred wood and piled up, blackened rocks cover the land, it becomes clear why campfires are prohibited in many areas of the park. The campfire is firmly locked in the romance of camping tradition, and the author is the first to admit that there is something special about sitting around a crackling fire on a cool evening in the mountains. But the camp stove cooks better, cleaner, and more evenly.

Let's look at a few styles and examine some statistics. Lightweight camp stoves burn white gasoline, butane, or alcohol. Presently, white-gas stoves made by Optimus, Svea, and Mountain Safety Research (MSR) are the most available and widely used. They are hard to beat for fast, efficient cooking. White-gas stoves produce a steady, hot flame, which is vital in a winter climate. They require a little nursing and priming to get them going, but once the burning plate heats up, you're in business. Although this type of stove is the most expensive to purchase, it is the cheapest to operate. Alcohol-burning stoves have been somewhat overlooked as quality items. They are cheaper to purchase than white-gas stoves and are frequently sold in a cook set/stove combination. The flame is hot but not very good for cold-weather cooking. Stoves that utilize butane cannisters are among the most popular. There are a number of makes and models available, including those made by Primus, Bluet, and the so-called Gerry Stove. These stoves are light and compact, easy to operate, and relatively inexpensive. They require no priming, just the turn of a valve and a match. The author recommends these stoves for camping in spring through fall on the basis of eight years of trouble-free, efficient summer cooking with the same stove. They are the least expensive, easiest to use, and probably the safest. One final note that should not be overlooked is that of the one hundred backcountry campsites in RMNP, more than forty of these sites are restricted to stoves only. If you plan to camp in this park or, for that matter, any of the national parks, and you do not own a camp stove, your camping options will be severely limited. Also, if you are unlucky enough to experience an extended rainstorm, beginning about the time you are fixing dinner, you can cook just outside your tent under the rain fly with a camp stove.

Cook kits for backpacking are generally lightweight and require less space. The small, traditional Boy Scout-type cook set contains cup, plate, fry pan, and small kettle. This type of kit is inexpensive and compact, but usually lacks adequate volume for more than one or two people. A slightly larger size cook set consists of one pot within another, with a lid, sometimes Teflon-coated, which can serve as a frying pan or plate. The larger size of this set is not necessarily a disadvantage, since food, pot grips, toilet paper, cups, and so on can be packed inside to conserve space.

One type of cook kit is designed to cook in layers. The individual pots in the kit are designed to sit on top of each other, with a camp stove set in its base. This method is quite popular for winter camping, since this arrangement saves space and keeps food warm until served. As the layered cook kit resembles the Leaning Tower of Pisa, campers utilizing it should remember that the higher center of gravity makes it more unstable. Level ground is an obvious prerequisite.

Cleaning pots and pans is a necessary evil, at home or in the woods. Here are some suggestions that will help. When cooking foods such as eggs, Teflon coating is a veritable godsend. A small Chore-boy cleaning pad easily removes baked-on residue. When using soap, try to secure the biodegradable type. The same soap can be used for the hands as well as the dishes. When using noncoated pots, a handful of sand rubbed on as an abrasive cleans well. But regardless of the cleaning agent used, avoid pouring the residue into the lakes and streams. Do your washing a reasonable distance away.

For those who cook on open fires, the problems increase. Not only is there invariably baked-on residue to clean inside, but also outside, where ash and soot collect. Coating the outside of a pot, especially the bottom, with a bar of soap, makes the collected grit wash off more easily.

Some miscellaneous items related to meal preparation deserve mention. A good pair of pot grippers is a convenient item to have around. It easily clamps on and off pots, eliminating the need for a gloved hand, especially over fires. Food tubes, another relatively recent innovation, consist of small plastic tubes, capped on one end, open on the other. Foods such as margarine, honey, ketchup, and cooking oil can be easily put into the opened end of the tube. When filled, the open end is folded and sealed with a plastic clip. To use, simply squeeze the contents out as you desire and recap.

Cleaning them isn't a problem since they open enough to get a dish towel inside.

Salt, pepper, and other spices can be conveniently carried in small, 35-mm film containers. These cannisters, familiar to all photographers, can also be utilized for carrying salt tablets, aspirin, freeze-dried coffee, emergency fire-starting tinder, and matches. If you so desire, caps can be made totally watertight by sealing them with candle drippings.

CLOTHING

Although clothing is more critical in winter, it is an important consideration in summer and fall as well. Hypothermia or exposure is a very real danger to the unprepared. (See chapter 4.) Here are a few suggestions about what to look for in good mountaineering clothing. Keep in mind that the purpose of clothing is to prevent excessive heat loss. On many summer days, even at higher altitudes, a T-shirt may be sufficient during daylight hours. But always remember to prepare for changing conditions. The T-shirt you comfortably wore to an alpine lake during the day will be insufficient when, in even a slight breeze, the dampness of perspiration drains heat from your body. The sun that you were inadvertently depending on for comfort will provide less and less warmth as it sinks toward the horizon. And if the sky should cloud up, the source of radiant heat is essentially lost. For the overnight camper this is not a problem, since he has probably brought along warm clothing to deal with the dropping temperatures of evening. But the hiker who walks a little slower than expected to his destination and returns late, with only a T-shirt for warmth, may spend some uncomfortable hours getting home.

All hikers should be aware of the concept of dressing in layers. Rather than bringing along one very warm article of clothing, such as a down jacket, bring instead a wool or a turtleneck shirt, a synthetic or down vest, and a Windbreaker. It is a lot easier to reach a comfortable level of insulation by adding or taking off a little bit at a time. With a jacket, it is either on or off. But this is not to say that your down jacket should be left at home. When packed in a stuff sack, it takes up little space, and you may want it for extra warmth in the chilly evening.

It is especially good to have a warm, dry piece of clothing at the top of your pack to put on when you reach your campsite. Get out of a damp shirt as soon as possible. Damp socks and shirts can be put at the bottom of a sleeping bag at night to help dry them out for the next day. Boots too can be put in your sleeping bag. Even if they are still damp with sweat in the morning, at least they won't feel like ice cubes when you put them on.

Rain gear is another necessary item. Though such gear is occasionally necessary because of rain, it may cause some discomfort due to condensation of body moisture within the garment. To illustrate this, we can return to the example of the waterproof tent. When body moisture confronts non-porous material, it collects on that material. This usually isn't a problem if you are waiting out a thunderstorm in a rain suit or poncho. But with exercise such as hiking, perspiration is more and more a factor. Sometimes it comes down to a choice between being wet from rain or wet from sweat.

A poncho is a good item to carry because it can be worn over both the body and backpack. Side snaps help avoid flapping and billowing in wind. A waterproof poncho, worn over your pack, keeps you drier, since it touches your body in fewer places. When worn without a pack, the poncho will hang over the shoulders. Any dampness is the result of condensation inside.

Rain suits have the advantage of protecting the whole body (except hands and feet) from rain, thus keeping the wind from blowing moisture in from the sides, as with a poncho. But they restrict movement more and are usually more expensive. If you wear a poncho and worry about getting your legs wet, rain chaps are available. These items slip on each leg and tie to the belt. They are loose to allow freedom of movement and to prevent excessive condensation.

There is a material presently utilized in the production of mountaineering equipment called Gore-Tex. Its most notable property is that it is effectively waterproof, yet breathable.

Though expensive, it is the best rain gear material currently available.

FOOD AND WATER

Nourishment on the trail affects your ability to hike comfortably, as well as your physical well-being. Being full doesn't necessarily mean being well nourished. This isn't of such great importance on summer overnights, but does become important on longer trips, especially in colder weather. A ravenous appetite for sugars and salts while camping isn't just a coincidence. The need for energy from nutrients is dramatically elevated on a strenuous trip, and one should plan menus accordingly. Frequently we are concerned about eating too many calories; on the trail the concern should be with the other extreme.

A very fine energy food for the trail is a substance popularly known as "gorp." There are many recipes for this delight, but it is basically a simple combination of high-energy foods, like chocolate chips, beer nuts or cashews, raisins, coconut, and the like. This amalgam is often carried in a zip-lock plastic bag, in the side pocket of the pack for easy access. Candy bars and hard candy are also popular energy foods that can be carried in a shirt pocket and consumed every so often without stopping to rummage through a pack. Tropical chocolate bars are especially handy in hot weather, since they melt less easily. Dried fruits also provide a nourishing and tasty trail food. Keep in mind that your food may not be safe simply stuck away in your pack. Various rodents that inhabit the park, such as pine martens and weasels, are excellent burglars. Make absolutely sure that any meat items are securely wrapped in plastic containers. Zip-lock sandwich bags or bread sacks are quite suitable. Thus wrapped, it is best to place the food in a stuff sack, and hang it from a tree branch.

The question of what to eat in camp is determined by each individual's tastes and preferences. But perhaps we ought to compare canned and perishable foods with food that is freeze-dried. Unfortunately, one thing that stands out is the cost difference. Freeze-dried foods are expensive. But for many the benefit derived from these products outweighs the expense. Since the moisture has been removed, they are extremely light. Because of this, they are virtually unperishable when retained in their packaging. They are easy to prepare and tasty. There is no dish washing involved with some freeze-dried products, since a pouch is provided for mixing the food with hot water. Each supplier of these products offers many meals from which to choose. Some very good dishes include shrimp creole, lasagna, beef stew, beef stroganoff, and turkey tetrazzini, as well as a myriad of side dishes, breakfasts, snacks, and beverages. Almost all backpacking stores, as well as grocery stores, stock freeze-dried food. Although such food items are not necessarily marketed as camping food in grocery stores, they are completely suitable and generally less expensive than products found in mountaineering stores. The next time you are in a grocery store, spend a few minutes and locate the types of lightweight meals that are available. It will be time well spent.

For the most part, drinking water is not a problem in the park. Most mountain streams are pure, but it is wise to avoid water in streams at lower elevations, as well as those that are not fast moving. Normally speaking, a one-quart bottle will provide you with an adequate supply of water to reach any destination. By the time that is expended, you will be high enough to start replenishing your supply out of mountain streams.

MISCELLANEOUS ITEMS

The discussion of equipment will close with this section on miscellaneous camping items. While some of the following are strictly optional, other items should always be brought for safety and personal comfort.

Although not critical under most circumstances, it's a good idea to get used to carrying a map and compass. Equally important is the knowledge of how to use both if the situation warrants it. A map comes in handy when there is a question as to distance covered on a trip, landmark names, elevations, where to expect water, and dozens of other questions. For those who think the only use of a compass is to point north, it would be wise to read up on the skill and sport of orienteering. Several good guides to the map and compass are listed in the Bibliography.

Insects can be exasperating and unwelcome companions on any hiking trip. One of the most unwelcome is the mosquito. Insect repellants containing diethyl-metatoluamide are among the most effective. Ticks are apparently most repelled by preparations containing dimethyl phthalate or diethyltoluamide. (Procedures for dealing with ticks will be discussed along with first aid and medical disorders in chapter 4.)

Some mountains in the park, although not technically difficult to climb, have steep snowfields for part or all of the summer. For backpackers who venture to such areas, an ice ax is valuable, but only with knowledge about its proper use. Since manuals exist on technical mountaineering a full treatment of ice ax technique is unwarranted here. (Consult the Bibliography.) But very briefly, an ice ax enables its carrier to perform a *self-arrest* in the event of a fall on steep snow. A self-arrest is essentially a series of motions the sliding climber goes through, culminating in forcing the pointed tip of the axhead into the snow, thereby stopping the slide. Those who aspire to climb mountains of greater than average difficulty may want to check with park officials on the advisability of carrying an ice ax on their climbs.

These final items are among those that you will want to bring, for one reason or another, on almost every trip. They include a first-aid kit, camera and extra film, pocket knife (Swiss Army type recommended), plastic trash bag, toilet paper, flashlight and extra batteries, a good quality pair of sunglasses, high altitude sunburn ointment, and extra matches. Many of these items can be placed in zip-lock plastic bags for convenience.

To conclude, there are many pieces of equipment the novice backpacker may want eventually, but can't afford all at once. A good quality pair of boots that fits properly is the first order of business. The other so-called big purchase items, such as tent, sleeping bag, and pack, can be rented until you are ready to buy your own. The incidentals can be accumulated a little at a time. Your equipment doesn't have to be the best money can buy, but quality should be commensurate with how much you expect to use it.

SUMMER/FALL EQUIPMENT CHECKLIST

These items are usually carried by backpackers. Some are optional, while others you should bring along every time. It is not meant to be the final word, but only a reminder.

pack
sleeping bag and pad
tent or sufficient shelter
cooking equipment
camp stove (extra fuel as needed)*
matches
sufficient food
trail snacks*
appropriate clothing
light gloves*
flashlight (extra batteries as needed)
first-aid kit
water bottle(s)
toilet paper
biodegradable soap*
sunglasses
camera and film*
pocket knife
small plastic trash bags
rain gear
ice ax*
accessory cord
map
compass*

*These are optional items, which you should bring according to need.

Chapter 4

Physical Conditioning and Personal Safety

There have been songs too great to be described in words, and there have been griefs upon which I have dared not dwell, and with these in mind I say climb if you will. But remember that courage and strength are nought without prudence and that a momentary negligence may destroy the happiness of a lifetime. Do nothing in haste, look well to each step, and think from the beginning what may be the end.

–Edward Whymper
Zurich, 1898

ACCLIMATIZATION

Denver is called the Mile High City. At 5,280 feet above sea level, it sits almost 7,000 feet below the Alpine Visitor Center at the top of Trail Ridge Road. Keep in mind that with the increased elevation of the mountains, there will be relatively less oxygen for your body to utilize. Frequently, first-time park visitors remark that they have difficulty catching their breath. The high altitude causes them to be tired and sluggish. This is part of the process of acclimatization–of adapting to thinner air. This process, which normally takes about two to three days, involves inhaling a greater volume of air, extracting and transporting to the body tissues a higher percentage of oxygen, and increasing the efficiency of utilization of this oxygen by body tissues. After two or three days at higher altitude, the body can, through various biochemical adaptations, permit normal metabolism despite the lack of oxygen. Altitude tolerance seems to be lost at about the same rate, two or three days. However, most people acclimatize more easily after their first experience at higher altitudes and find the transition less difficult on successive visits.

There is a tendency for hikers on a limited time schedule to race off immediately, hitting as many trails, lakes, and mountains as possible. But be assured that hiking will be much more pleasant if you work up to this pace with some easier hikes. The Nymph-Dream-Emerald Lake trail, for example, is good for starters. Others include the Cub Lake-Pool trail, and hikes to Mills Lake, Calypso Cascades, and Specimen Mountain. An afternoon of photography while wandering on the tundra off Trail Ridge Road is also a pleasant and effective way to adapt to the altitude. If you choose your own hike from the trails described in this book, consider the distance covered as well as the elevation rise you will encounter. Three miles along the relatively flat trail in Wild Basin is not quite like three miles up the side of a mountain. Acclimatization implies adapting to both the altitude and the exercise. Quite possibly the novice hiker will be sore and a bit stiff the morning after that first hike. That's the time to get out and do it again. Each time it will become easier. Once you are adapted to the altitude and the hiking, half the fun, not half the pain, is getting there.

HIKING IN THE MOUNTAINS

In hiking, pace is everything. Eventually, every hiker discovers a comfortable pace for both steep and level terrain. At the beginning of a hike, especially if the initial section of trail is steep, walking may be uncomfortable and you may feel like you will burn out within the hour. But you will reach a plateau of sorts within ten to twenty minutes. This will vary according to conditioning. This is popularly called "getting your walking legs." After this level has been reached, it is easier, both psychologically and physically, to crank out the miles.

Hikers usually use one of two basic styles. Some hikers really turn it on and make good time, but periodically stop to rest along the trail. If you are in shape and want to reach your destination quickly, then you might consider this method.

However, it is the author's experience that employing a slower pace with as few stops as possible is the most comfortable way of walking with a full pack. The more you stop and the longer you rest, the longer it will take you to find your "walking legs." You should strive for an even, rhythmic pace, perhaps thinking of a song to match each step, much like a metronome. Some people carry hiking sticks and work out a rhythm, such as two steps for each time the stick is planted on the trail. The method is less important than the effect: to establish and maintain an even pace.

Bear in mind that your pace will vary as the trail ascends and descends. No matter what the grade of the trail, don't fight it. On rocky paths, especially when steep, you should look carefully where you place each step. Avoid stepping up on rocks as much as possible. Make the walk as gradual as the lay of the land permits. On a very short hike these considerations are inconsequential. But on a trip of seven to ten miles one way, it is possible to climb hundreds of feet higher than your hiking companions by continually stepping up and down along the trail. More importantly, it is difficult to maintain an even pace while doing so.

Steep trails are constructed with switchbacks for two important reasons. First, a trail that goes straight down, parallel with the fall line of the hill, will be washed out and become a small gulley.* Second, it is easier to switchback up a hill even though the distance walked is longer. Hikers who fancy themselves as speed demons in the mountains and cut switchbacks at every opportunity are not only violating park regulations, and causing environmental damage, but are also defeating themselves physically. In addition, dozens of hikers are lost as a result of taking shortcuts. It is rather easy to become disoriented in a forest without reference points for direction. So stick to the trail and maintain a steady pace. You'll save energy and probably time as well.

While hiking, it may be helpful to remember that "a watched pot never boils." If you find yourself on a long summit ridge where the top is visible, don't look up continually to check on your progress. Concentrate instead on where each

*A *fall line* is the natural downhill course between two points on a slope.

boot is being placed, particularly on boulder-strewn sections of the trail. Toward the end of an arduous climb, when energy reserves are dwindling, it can be psychologically devastating to look up continually. It is best to pick out a spot a few hundred feet away and work toward that as a goal. When that spot has been reached, pick another an equal distance higher up and so on. This helps alleviate the feeling of being defeated by the size of the mountain. The same is true for more level trail hikes. Pick out some places along the way as goals or perhaps for preplanned rest stops. For example, along the Fern Lake trail, The Pool and Fern Falls are convenient and scenic rest stops. The Pool is roughly the halfway point, and Fern Falls is about halfway between The Pool and Fern Lake.

Some hikers plan their trips so as to avoid returning on the same trail. Obviously, you will be able to see more country that way. If your destination offers an alternate return route, it might be more enjoyable to explore new scenery on the way back. Some elect to travel one-way between two connecting trailheads, such as the trail between Bear Lake and the Fern Lake parking area. This, however, requires two vehicles in the hiking party.

Cross-country travel, without the benefit of a trail, ought to be undertaken by the beginning hiker only if he is well acquainted with the maps of an area and knows how to read them. If you decide to travel without a trail keep a few things in mind. Foremost among these is to remember to stay together. You should intentionally separate from your hiking companions *only* if an emergency develops, such as an injury. While traveling above timberline without a trail, it is wise to avoid traveling single file. Since the tundra is a delicate environment, hiking single file increases the impact. Before commencing on an off-trail hike, be sure you have the appropriate maps and a compass.

MEDICAL AND SAFETY CONSIDERATIONS

The mountains are a different world than many of its visitors are used to. Over one-fourth of Rocky Mountain National Park is alpine tundra at over 11,500 feet. This environment is characterized by more ultraviolet light, less oxygen, frequent afternoon electric storms, fluctuating temperatures, and steep mountains. Snowstorms have been seen in Estes Park on the fourth of July. The backpacker and hiker can exist in this environment in complete safety and harmony, but it requires an awareness of what is happening around him. Since accidents can happen to you, a member of your party, or someone you meet on the trail, a good first-aid kit is of utmost importance.

Every hiking party ought to have at least one first-aid kit and at least one person who can use it effectively. For obvious reasons, it does not need to be a portable paramedic station. Certainly, any injury requiring specialized medical paraphernalia can't be treated on the trail anyway. A good mountaineering first-aid kit ought to be built around the premise of stabilizing an injured victim until transportation by competent rescuers can be arranged. Consider these contents for your first-aid kit:

2" x 2" and 4" x 4" gauze (principal item)
adhesive tape
Band-Aids
moleskin
safety pins
triangular bandages
tweezers
sunburn ointment
aspirin and salt tablets
antiseptic prep pads
Ace bandage
compression bandage

In the event of a bad sprain or a broken bone in the mountains, makeshift splints can be fashioned out of anything, including branches and ice axes. It is always advisable to hike with at least two in a party. In the event of injury there will be someone to go for help.

If an individual has fallen and there is even a remote suspicion of a break, especially if the victim is unconscious, it is essential that he is not moved. Moving a person with neck or back fractures can cause permanent paralysis. Excessively moving a broken limb can exacerbate already damaged tissue, vessels, and nerves.

Another reason to avoid solo trips is the insidious nature

of *hypothermia,* or exposure. Though hypothermia is more frequent in colder temperatures than are common in the park in summer, it can happen. Hypothermia is a condition in which the body is unable to maintain its normal temperature. It is caused by a depletion of bodily nutrients in an environment where the victim is subjected to greater heat loss than the body can replace. If the heat loss goes unchecked, it is like pulling a cork at the bottom of a barrel. Heat will eventually drain to the point of no return. Five ways heat is lost from the body are:

- *Evaporation:* of sweat from the skin.
- *Respiration:* inhaling cool air and exhaling warm air.
- *Conduction:* contact with anything cooler than the skin.
- *Convection:* air passing over the body, drawing off the warm layer of air trapped by clothing.
- *Radiation:* The greatest cause of heat loss; the greater the difference between environmental and body temperature, the more exaggerated the rate.

Hypothermia may develop due to: (1) lack of sufficient body nutrients for energy; (2) insufficient insulation by clothing; (3) extended exposure to a chilly, damp environment; (4) exposure to wind; or (5) inability to recognize symptoms of hypothermia.

Visible symptoms of hypothermia are clear and usually unmistakable. Initially, the victim is drowsy and uncommunicative. Inability to control shivering and maintain muscle movement is followed by confusion and apparent exhaustion. The body temperature continues a downward spiral unless you can stop it. The victim rarely realizes what is happening because, as body temperature decreases, the brain becomes numb to stimulus.

Treatment for hypothermia is heat from any source. Since there won't be a convenient sauna in woods, you must depend on hot liquids, especially those with sugar. If a sleeping bag is available, strip the victim of his clammy, wet clothing and get him into the bag. Another person inside the bag can transmit radiant heat and make sure the victim stays awake. If a thermometer is carried in a first-aid kit, then the person's temperature can be monitored. Should hypothermia be suspected in any member of your party, check the person, ask questions, and look for shivering and damp clothing. If each member in your group is aware of the weather and each other, hypothermia can be stopped before it ever starts.

Mountain sickness is a disorder which, though not serious, can cause discomfort to the stricken mountaineer. It typically strikes people who arrive from very low altitudes and immediately attempt hard exertion at elevations in excess of 8,000 feet (a persuasive argument for allowing a two- to three-day acclimatization period). Initial symptoms include drowsiness, weakness, chills, headache, occasional nausea, and possible dizziness. Rest is the best treatment. Symptoms usually disappear within twenty-four to forty-eight hours, but the hiker should resume walking only on the easiest trails for a period after symptoms and discomfort disappear.

Although *pulmonary edema* is quite uncommon, it is included here as a possibility at high altitude. Generally speaking, it occurs, like mountain sickness, in people who make a rapid ascent from low-lying areas to elevations in excess of 8,000 to 9,000 feet. Some physicians suggest that mountain residents who have spent up to three weeks at low elevations and return to the mountains are more susceptible than first-time visitors. Pulmonary edema is caused by excessive fluid that collects in the lungs, thus interfering with adequate respiration. Consequently, one of the symptoms includes bubbling sounds when one listens to the chest, especially when the victim is sitting or standing up. The victim typically displays shortness of breath, even at rest, a rapid pulse, weakness, a slightly elevated temperature, and an incessant cough. This is a serious disorder and although the principal treatment involves retreating to a lower elevation, a physician should be contacted.

The sun can be a problem to the unprepared mountaineer. If you venture to the high country in the spring and early summer when snow is plentiful, bring sunglasses. The glare of snowfields, especially at higher altitudes on sunny days, can result in "sunburned" eyes or *photopthalmia.* This condition, also known as snow-blindness, involves eye irritation, with symptoms of dryness and the sensation of sand in the eyes. These symptoms may develop within hours of exposure. The condition, however, heals spontaneously within a few days. Opthalmic ointments recommended by a physician may be helpful in easing discomfort. During this period, bright sunlight should be avoided, and a dark environment is most comfortable.

It is advisable to carry sun creams and preparations to help block the sun's rays. Each individual probably has a fair idea of the degree of sunburn he can expect during particular durations of outdoor activities such as hiking or skiing. Realize, though, that in the higher and thinner air sunburn will occur more quickly than you expect.

Although ticks are most common in RMNP during May and June, they are found throughout the summer and occasionally into fall. They are frequently contracted while walking through sagebrush or similar vegetation. Finding a tick on one's body certainly isn't pleasant, but it isn't a cause for panic. If it has attached itself (often they will not have) start by applying a few drops of lighter fluid, insect repellant, nail polish remover, or parasite ointment to the creature. If that doesn't convince it to cease and desist, then gently pull it out with tweezers or fingers, being careful not to crush it. Antiseptic (from your first-aid kit) should be applied to the site of attachment after removal. If the head breaks off during removal, it probably would be wise to see a physician. *Colorado tick fever* is a possibility in such cases. Colorado tick fever, caused by a virus transmitted by the tick, can result even if the head of the tick is unbroken in removal. Symptoms include headaches of varying severity, fever, muscle aches, and occasionally a rash.

Rocky Mountain spotted fever is actually more common outside of Colorado. Its symptoms are similar to tick fever, but they are of greater severity and duration. A vaccine is available, and treatment with antibiotics is very effective.

Treatment for rattlesnake bites does not warrant discussion in a manual for hiking in Rocky Mountain National Park, since you won't see any here. Rattlers have a definite altitude range and are not found this high.

MOUNTAIN ETIQUETTE AND COMMON SENSE

It is hoped that the reader won't view this section as a lecture. There are some things that ought to be intuitively accepted as unsafe or disrespectful. By following some basic rules, hiking and camping in Rocky Mountain National Park or elsewhere can be more enjoyable for all concerned.

First and foremost is litter. There is nothing new under the sun that can be said about this problem, but no discussion of mountain etiquette would be complete without it. Litter around a campsite is aesthetically deleterious to an otherwise beautiful mountain vista. People who prefer to dwell amid their own garbage are pathetic; those who force others to do so are an outrage. The various wrappings and packagings of food brought into a campsite can be easily packed out. On your backpacking trips, bring a plastic bag along to deal with litter. It certainly isn't demeaning to pick up someone else's trash while you are at it. Be proud that you have helped keep one small part of this good land as natural as it was made.

Silence has an intrinsic beauty all its own. Perhaps it is because modern man lives in a noise-ridden world that quiet offers such relief. Or maybe it is that we are so used to noise that, for some, it is difficult to feel comfortable without it. Noise is regarded by many as an environmental pollutant. Therefore, just as you avoid littering your campsite, you should be aware that there may be other campers in the vicinity. Noise from a campsite can easily carry across a mountain lake and destroy the peace that many backpackers are there to enjoy. On the trail, there is an advantage of quiet beyond mere aesthetics. If you want to see any wildlife in the park, you will have difficulty if you announce your presence to every creature within earshot. People who wander the mountains, shouting aloud to hear their own echo, would be well advised to purchase a cheap tape recorder instead. Crying out hello can too easily be interpreted as a call for help, especially when distance is such that distinguishing words is difficult.

Some people seem to possess a peculiar and untiring fascination with throwing rocks. Perhaps the habit begins when young, for many children throw rocks into rivers and lakes with abandon. But when rocks are thrown and kicked off mountaintops, ridges, high trails, or virtually anywhere, it is no longer innocent fun. This can be a real danger to people the rock-throwers do not expect to be below them. As a member of a local mountain rescue team, the author has seen sad evidence of at least one person's negligence with this supposedly innocent fun.

Sliding on snow for entertainment or as a means of descending a mountain can be a lot of fun. But always remember to look before you leap. Is the slope gradual enough that you could stop if you had to? Can you see if there are rocks at the bottom or on the snowfield? Does the steepness require an ice ax to descend safely? If you are on a glacier, do you know if there are crevasses in your path? Use a little common sense and the worst thing that will come of it will be a wet seat.

In addition to the danger of sliding on steep snow is the possibility of avalanches. These are more common in the winter, but they can occur anytime in the high country, especially where drifted cornices overhang steep snowbanks. The earlier in the spring it is, the more caution you should use. Play it safe and avoid areas that appear dangerous.

Animals are part of the beauty of the park. It's natural to want to get a close look if possible. But there are a few points to keep in mind. Rodents in the park have been occasionally known to be infected with plague. For obvious reasons, any dead creature should not be handled under any circumstances. Because of the danger of being bitten, squirrels and chipmunks should not be fed by hand. It is also unwise because the food you feed animals attributes to their dependence on human beings for handouts, altering their natural feeding patterns and habits. Save those beer nuts for yourself, and let the chipmunks play their part in the ecosystem. If you come across a baby animal in hiding, it probably hasn't been abandoned. You're probably frightening it into a seizure by your presence. Simply consider yourself enriched by the experience and leave quietly.

Finally, perhaps the greatest wisdom you can carry into the mountains is an understanding of your own capabilities and limitations. An experienced hiker should be able to turn back, either because of severe weather or the failing endurance of hiking party members. It is difficult to deny yourself the summit of a mountain because of an electric storm that may be gone in ten minutes–or three hours. But lightning is dangerous and should be respected. Avoid ridges and other exposed places during lightning. Metal items such as ice axes and pack frames (which have been known to vibrate and glow with electricity) should be stashed away from your bivouac.

Weather, which in the morning seems benign, can turn into driving drizzle or snow by afternoon. Fog can disorient hikers who are without compass or off the trail. Wind can make some summit ridges almost impassable. And nighttime can come on with remarkable speed. The one preventive measure for all of these contingencies is simply to stop and take an occasional look around you.

Sometimes those members of a hiking or climbing party least able to make it are the last ones to admit it. Although they are considerably more pleasant to be with than prophets of doom who predict death before the summit is reached, their silence is inappropriate to the situation. It's best to cast pride to the wind and mention any ailments that may affect your ability to hike. It will be to no one's benefit if your companions have to carry you down.

It is inadvisable to attempt technical climbs without proper equipment or experience. Those who view climbing strictly in terms of courage and not as a sport, which must be practiced and perfected, should remember that discretion is the better part of valor.

It should be noted that this chapter is not intended to cause potential visitors to Rocky Mountain National Park to remain in the lowlands. This discussion has been included to assist the hiker in recognizing and reacting to some mountaineering contingencies. Ignorance may be bliss, but it invites trouble. Common sense and awareness are good preventive measures in avoiding problems.

Chapter 5

Campsites and Park Regulations

Most of this chapter is based on material available from Rocky Mountain National Park headquarters. The regulations outlined generally refer to June through September. Some distinctions should be made between campgrounds and campsites. Generally speaking, *campgrounds* are those areas associated with vehicle camping. *Campsites* usually refer to those areas reached by trail, and are marked by two-letter codes on the maps in part three. The inevitable changes in park regulations and campground/campsite numbers will be reflected in future editions of this book. This chapter is included to acquaint the camper with Rocky Mountain National Park camping areas. Also, keep in mind that campsite classifications of "fire" or "stoves only" may vary from June to September depending on the frequency of visitation. This can easily be checked at the backcountry office.

BACKCOUNTRY CAMPING

In the past few years, intensified use of the backcountry by increasing numbers of campers has resulted in damage to some of the more popular camping spots. To protect the fragile resources of Rocky Mountain National Park, a written Backcountry Use Permit is required for all overnight stays other than in campgrounds accessible by roads. Permits may be obtained by mail ahead of time, or in person at the time of arrival. They may be obtained in person from the East and West District backcountry offices and at each headquarters. The permit costs no more than your time.

Reservations are available for backcountry campsites year-round, and can be made by writing to: Reservations, Backcountry Office, Rocky Mountain National Park, Estes Park, Colorado 80517. They can be made by phone at (303) 586-2371 during the nonsummer months (October through May). During the summer, if you wish to receive your permit by mail, indicate this in your request.

Holders of Backcountry Use Permits are requested to notify a ranger if unable to make use of all the time on the permit. This will allow issuance of a permit to others for those unused days. Since demand exceeds the sites available, please do your part to help.

A permit tag is issued to the party leader, and should be attached to his pack. The tag must be shown to backcountry patrol personnel on request. When camp is made, the tag is attached to the tent. The same permit is required for all technical mountain climbing. Technical climbing includes all climbing with ropes and other aids. The permit entitles you to camp only in those campsites and on those dates specified. Campsites are located on sites that are more able to withstand the wear and tear of camping. To camp elsewhere only spreads the impact to areas that recover less easily. Parties are limited to seven people. Parties of eight to twenty fall into the "group" category (see section on "Backcountry Group Camping").

Backcountry camping is limited to seven nights during June, July, August, and September. An additional fifteen nights is permitted between October 1 and May 31. You may remain three days at each campsite before moving to a different area. If you plan to do cross-country zone camping, your stay is limited to two days in each zone, and you must move your camp at least one mile each day.

Wood fires may be built *only* in metal fire rings. Where metal rings are not provided, campers must use containerized fuel stoves. These sites are designated "stoves only," and fires other than stoves are not allowed.

All trash must be packed out, and never buried, burned, or

tossed in toilet pits. If others have been careless, please help by removing their litter.

With the exception of horses, domestic animals are not permitted in the backcountry. The presence of domestic animals frightens away wildlife that you and other hikers enjoy.

Remember, you are in a wilderness area. Willingly accept the change of surroundings and the few discomforts associated with camping and hiking. You came seeking a quality wilderness experience. To alter any part of the park for creature comforts can only lower the quality of the wilderness.

Observe the following conservation practices:

1. Anything that is obtrusive or will modify the terrain should be left at the roadhead.

2. Avoid polluting lakes and streams. Place water for washing dishes or yourself in a container, and use it away from the source. Dispose of wash water away from the lake or stream.

3. Where no outhouses are present, disposal of human waste can become a problem. Select a spot at least one hundred feet from any water source, and dig a hole six inches deep, if possible preserving the sod. You can use a small, lightweight garden trowel, or else your boot heel. After use, fill the hole with loose soil, topped by sod. Nature will do the rest.

4. Stay on the trail, thus minimizing your impact. Shortcutting not only damages the fragile vegetation, but quickly leads to water erosion, which can wash out whole sections of trail.

5. Observe wildlife from a distance. All wild animals will protect themselves, their young, and their territory from danger. Even the bite of a squirrel or chipmunk can be painful, and may transmit disease.

6. Trees grow slowly at high altitudes, so go easy on them. Use a small fire, where permitted, or else a stove. Let your fires burn down to white ash so fireplaces can be kept clean. Never leave a fire unattended. Campfires have been

known to retain hot embers hours after smoke is visible or heat can be felt. When you put out a campfire, douse it well with water, stir the ashes, and then repeat. A quart of water and a little dirt will not extinguish most campfires. When you are finished, the ash ought to resemble mud and be cool enough to sift through the fingers.

7. The mountainous backcountry environment contains many hazards not commonly encountered. These include: slipping on snowfields; falling into turbulent streams; mountain-climbing without proper experience or equipment; traveling in violent lightning, wind, or snowstorms; and encounters with wildlife. Any of these can cause serious injury and set back your trip. If in doubt consult a ranger.

8. When fishing, obtain current fishing regulations, as park regulations differ somewhat from Colorado state regulations.

BACKCOUNTRY GROUP CAMPING

Demand for backcountry campsites by groups and organizations is growing rapidly, both locally and nationwide. In order to provide a worthwhile experience for those entering the backcountry, certain guidelines are necessary. All groups are reminded that park visitors seek the backcountry to find solitude and tranquility. Group leaders are requested to see that their group does not destroy others' enjoyment of that setting. Groups are expected to comply with all backcountry regulations. Below are further regulations pertaining specifically to group camping:

1. A *group* is any party of eight or more people traveling together. Groups are limited to a maximum of twenty people, including counselors, guides, and other leaders. Groups are not permitted to break into smaller parties and occupy individual sites in a given campsite area. During the winter months, groups are limited to a maximum of fifteen persons, and may not camp in designated group sites. See the pamphlet *Winter Backcountry Use*, available at park headquarters.

2. Both the organization's name and address, and the leader's name appear on the Backcountry Use Permit.
3. Groups are limited to three nights camping per area, and seven nights total from June to September. An additional fifteen nights is permitted between October 1 and May 31.
4. Sanitation is a particular problem with groups; please use the privies.
5. Because of the backcountry demand during July and August, local area groups should refrain from weekend trips during these months.
6. Designated group sites June through September are presently limited to specific sites at the following areas:
   - *East District*—Boulder Brook,** Battle Mountain,** Cut Bank, Finch Lake, Fern Lake, Lost Meadow,** Sandbeach Lake,** Thunder Lake,** Stormy Peaks**
   - *West District*—Big Meadow,** Chapin Group, Ditch Camp No. 3, Hague Creek,** Hallett Group, North Inlet,* Summerland, Tonahutu Group,* Junco, Red Gulch

CROSS-COUNTRY ZONE CAMPING

To take advantage of camping possibilities in the cross-country zones, a few special skills are necessary. As a result, there are regulations. This section deals only with summer cross-country zone camping.

Cross-country zones provide a minimum-impact type of camping for backpackers experienced in cross-country travel below tree line. Such camping is without maintained trails, and does not permit building fires. A camper planning to use the cross-country zones should be familiar with (and plan to use) a minimum-impact, no-trace style of camping. Since there are no trails in the cross-country zones, a map and compass may be needed to plot courses. At least one person in the party should have this skill. Cross-country zones are not as accessible as park areas near maintained trails. Since

*These are horse group camps. All campers using stock animals, please refer to pamphlet *Use of Private Saddle and Pack Stock* for special regulations. Horse group camps are available to hiking groups (maximum of twenty people) if not used by a horse group.

**These are "stoves only" campsites, with no fires allowed.

they are less frequently traveled, parties using the zones are advised to carry some emergency supplies and a well-stocked first-aid kit. All campers should refer to the *Overnight Backcountry Use* pamphlet for rules, regulations, and guidelines for backcountry overnight use.

Choice of campsite location in cross-country zones is left to the camper, provided he follows guidelines set up for this use:

1. There is a maximum of seven persons per party.
2. Campsites must be:
   a. Within the designated boundaries of the cross-country zone.
   b. Designated on the permit by the camper as to drainage and approximate elevation.
   c. At least one hundred feet from any water source.
   d. Out of sight and sound of other campers.
   e. Moved at least one mile each day. Camping is limited to two days total in any one zone.
   f. Established as stated on the permit. You must reach the proposed campsite location for the permit to be valid.
3. Open fires are not permitted. All cooking must be done with a containerized fuel stove.
4. All trash, including cigarette butts, must be packed out of the backcountry and disposed of properly.

Privies are not provided in cross-country zones, and human waste can be a problem if not disposed of correctly. Cross-country backpackers should use the "cat hole" method so that the waste will be broken down by bacteria in the upper six inches of soil. If not familiar with the technique, please read and follow the instructions printed on the summer *Overnight Backcountry Use* pamphlet.

Maps of the cross-country zones are available only at ranger stations and at the backcountry office at headquarters. If you are familiar with the cross-country zones, and know where you wish to camp, you may make a reservation ahead of time for a cross-country zone campsite. Refer to the

Overnight Backcountry Use pamphlet concerning reservations. If you are not familiar with the zones and their locations, you may obtain a cross-country zone permit at the backcountry office when you reach the park.

Backpackers using areas without trails should travel in a low-impact manner. Stepping from rock to rock whenever possible helps preserve fragile alpine flora. Traveling in a random, scattered manner rather than single-file avoids repeated trampling of vegetation and the establishment of multiple trails in any area. Remember this guideline when traveling from your campsite to the water source, and plan a different route each time. The general rule for all cross-country zone use is to leave no trace of your passage through an area. If all users of cross-country zones keep this idea foremost and camp accordingly, the zones will retain their "little used" appearance and appeal.

CAMPING FACILITIES AND REGULATIONS

There are five campgrounds in Rocky Mountain National Park, with over seven hundred campsites. Campgrounds are open during the summer months (late May to Labor Day). Space for camping is available at other times of the year, but water systems may not be in operation. Camping in park campgrounds is limited to seven nights, except at Longs Peak campground, where three nights is maximum. Camping, sleeping, and overnight parking in areas other than designated campsites is not permitted. Campsites are available on a first come basis; no reservations are available. All campgrounds fill up early in the day in July and August. Private campgrounds are available outside the park.

Campground regulations. There are no hookups available for trailers or other recreation vehicles at any of the park campgrounds. Many campgrounds are suitable for travel trailers, motor homes, and pickup campers, while other sites are the walk-in type, designed to accommodate only tent campers. Recreation vehicles may be accommodated in all campgrounds but the Longs Peak campground, where only tent camping is permitted.

Numbered campgrounds consist of an auto parking space,

a table, a fireplace, and an area for a tent or other equipment. Comfort stations (either modern or pit privy type), piped water, and trash receptacles are located conveniently in each campground. Sanitary dump stations are located at Moraine Park, Glacier Basin, and Timber Creek campgrounds.

Groups. Organized groups may make reservations for one of the group campsites in the Glacier Basin campground. In writing for group reservations, state the type of group, the number of people (if yours is a youth group, please state number of youths and names of adult sponsors), dates of arrival and departure, transportation (type and number of vehicles), and type of camping equipment you will use (number and size if you are using tents). An *organized group* is any group with a charter issued by a legislature or other governing body outlining the principles, functions, and structure of the group. Examples include: Boy Scouts, Girl Scouts, and groups officially sponsored by educational institutions and churches. Family groups, recreation vehicle caravan groups, and other park visitors must utilize regular campgrounds.

Showers and other facilities. No campgrounds in Rocky Mountain National Park have shower facilities. Showers are available in nearby villages and in commercial campgrounds outside the park. Doctors, groceries, camping supplies, service stations, and self-service laundries are available in the towns of Estes Park and Grand Lake. Public telephones are located at Moraine Park, Glacier Basin, and Aspenglen.

Firewood. Firewood is sold in bundles at campgrounds and at several locations outside the park. Gathering firewood within the park is prohibited.

Mail. Campers expecting personal mail can have it sent in care of General Delivery to the post office in either Estes Park (zip code 80517) or Grand Lake (zip code 80447).

Pets. Dogs, cats, and other pets are permitted in the campgrounds, provided they are on a leash or under control at all times. Pets are not permitted on trails or in areas away from roads or developments. Kennels are available in Estes Park and Granby.

Campfire programs. These are conducted regularly in the various campground amphitheaters during summer evenings by park ranger-naturalists. Printed schedules of these programs, guided nature walks and hikes, and other interpretive activities are available at campground offices, ranger stations, and visitor centers.

Hunting and firearms. The park is dedicated to the preservation of natural conditions for the enjoyment of visitors. Native wildlife is a primary park resource, and all hunting or the use of firearms and other weapons is prohibited. Park campgrounds may not be used as base camps for hunting outside the park.

Campgrounds. The following park campgrounds are available for summer camping:

1. *Moraine Park Campground* (elevation 8,200 feet): Located 1.0 mile west of Moraine Park visitor center off Bear Lake Road (7.0 miles west of Estes Park); 260 campsites, including walk-in campsites. Facilities include ranger station, modern comfort stations, sanitary dump station, public telephone, and campfire amphitheaters.

2. *Glacier Basin Campground* (elevation 8,500 feet): Located 9.0 miles west of Estes Park on the Bear Lake Road; 224 campsites, plus twenty-five for organized groups. Facilities include ranger station, sanitary dump station, modern comfort stations, public telephone, and campfire amphitheater.

3. *Aspenglen Campground* (elevation 9,500 feet): Located 5.0 miles west of Estes Park near the Fall River entrance; seventy campsites. Facilities include water and modern comfort stations, public telephone, and campfire amphitheater. (In winter, pit toilets are available, but there is no water or firewood. Water is available at that time at the Fall River entrance station nearby.)

4. *Longs Peak Campground* (elevation 9,500 feet): Tents only. Located 11.0 miles south of Estes Park and 1.0 mile west of the South Saint Vrain Highway (Colorado Route 7); thirty campsites. No pickup campers, trailers, or motor homes. This campground is located near the start of the

Longs Peak trail. Ranger station and modern comfort stations.

5. *Timbercreek Campground* (elevation 8,900 feet): Located 10.0 miles north of Grand Lake on Trail Ridge Road; 100 campsites. This is the only campground in the park on the west side of the continental divide. Has ranger station, modern comfort stations, sanitary dump station, and campfire amphitheater.

Part Three

Trail Guide to the Park

Topographical Maps

If you are unfamiliar with topographical maps, the first thing you should do is to acquaint yourself with the meaning of contour lines. These lines indicate specific elevations. For instance, you can locate the contour line for the 10,000-foot level and trace that same line all the way around a mountain. Wherever the line goes in that irregular circle indicates the same elevation. The closer the contour lines are to one another, the steeper the terrain. A good example of this can be seen in the Longs Peak map relating to chapter 6. The contour lines indicating the lay of the land on the east face of that mountain are actually touching each other, meaning a vertical wall. When you get used to "reading" the topography with these maps, you will be able to tell at a glance what kind of grade any given hike will present.

The maps used in this book are slightly larger in scale than the normal 7.5-minute series maps (7.5 minutes refers to the size of the area covered). The 7.5-minute maps utilize a contour interval of forty feet. This means that there is forty feet between each line on the map when translating it to actual elevation. With the exception of the Longs Peak map, the maps have a contour interval of eighty feet. Consequently, fewer lines are required to denote the elevation of a mountain on these larger scale maps.

The grey shading that you see on the maps of this book indicates forested areas. On actual topographical maps, the shading is green in color. This can be a valuable key in determining your exact location in the backcountry. Observe on the maps that the shading stops at the higher elevations. This indicates timberline. Below this area, lack of shading indicates a meadow or park. If you are trying to pinpoint your location, and you are standing in an open area with a prominent rock wall nearby, you should look for a bare spot in the shading near a series of dense contour lines on the map.

A key to all the symbols on topographical maps can be found below. Try to familiarize yourself with them. In addition, there is an index to the 7.5-minute topographical maps for the Rocky Mountain National Park area. This will help you visualize the relationship between the various maps. It is also suggested that you refer to the overall map of the park at the beginning of the book.

The following are topographical maps for various parts of the park. The trail guide section contains references to these maps, so refer to them often as you plan your hike.

SUPPLEMENTAL MAPS

The following U.S. Geological Survey maps may be helpful to you in planning your hikes. The names below refer to specific map sections, which can be obtained from park headquarters or U.S. Geological Survey offices. The relationship between these maps will be more clear if you refer to the map index below.

Chapter 6
Bear Lake, Glacier Gorge, and Longs Peak
- McHenrys Peak
- Longs Peak

Chapter 7
Wild Basin
- Isolation Peak
- Allens Park
- Longs Peak
- McHenrys Peak

Chapter 8

The Mummy Range

Trail Ridge
Estes Park
Commanche Peak
Pingree Park

Chapter 9

Along the Divide: Milner Pass to Big Horn Flats

Fall River Pass
Trail Ridge
Grand Lake
McHenrys Peak

Chapter 10

Across the Divide: The Grand Lake Drainage

Grand Lake
Shadow Mountain
McHenrys Peak
Isolation Peak

Chapter 11

The Never Summer Range and Upper Colorado River Valley

Mount Richthofen
Fall River Pass
Bowen Mountain
Grand Lake

CROSS-COUNTRY ZONES

As previously mentioned, the cross-country zones appear on the maps in this book, outlined with a dotted line, and coded. The cross-country zones for the areas in each chapter are as follows.

Chapter 6

Bear Lake, Glacier Gorge, and Longs Peak

Forest Canyon	1D

Chapter 7

Wild Basin

Hunters Creek	1G

Chapter 8

The Mummy Range

Poudre South Fork	1A
Stormy Peaks	2A
Mount Dickenson	1B
Dark Mountain	2B
Black Canyon	1C
Cascade Creek	1H
Hague Creek	2H
Chapin Creek	3H

Chapter 9

Along the Divide: Milner Pass to Big Horn Flats

Upper Onahu Creek	1K
Forest Canyon	1D

Chapter 10

Across the Divide: The Grand Lake Drainage

Nakai Peak	1L
Mount Patterson, West	2L
Mount Patterson, East	1M
Ptarmigan Creek	2M
Upper North Inlet	3M
Pettingell	4M
Mount Enentah	1N
Upper East Inlet	2N
Echo Creek	3N
Mount Bryant	1P

Chapter 11

The Never Summer Range and Upper Colorado River Valley

Skeleton Gulch	1J
Hell's Hip Pocket	2J

EXPLANATION

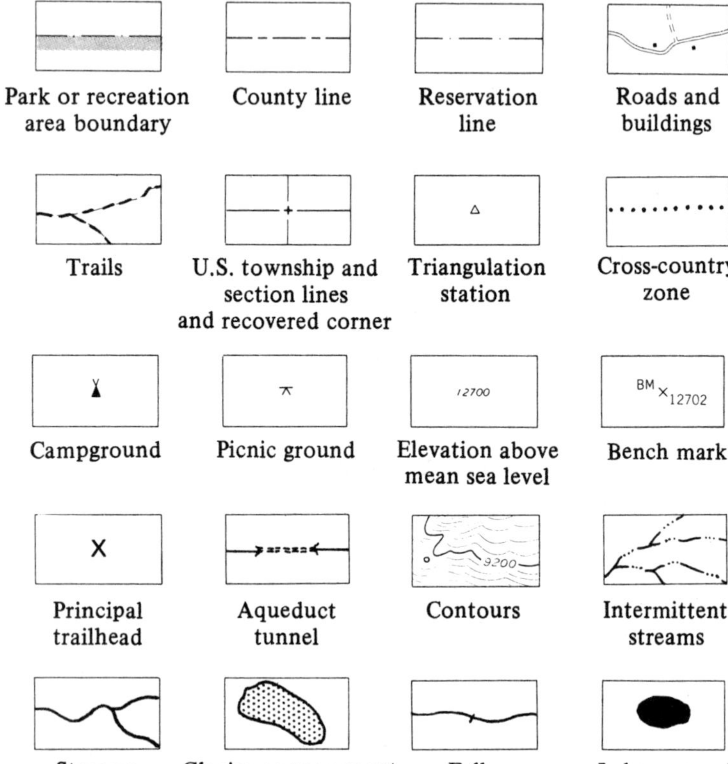

CLARK PEAK	CHAMBERS LAKE	COMANCHE PEAK	PINGREE PARK	CRYSTAL MOUNTAIN
MOUNT RICHTHOFEN 1957	FALL RIVER PASS 1958	TRAIL RIDGE 1957	ESTES PARK 1957	GLEN HAVEN
BOWEN MTN 1957	GRAND LAKE 1958	MCHENRYS PEAK 1957	LONGS PEAK 1957	PANORAMA PEAK
TRAIL MTN 1957	SHADOW MOUNTAIN 1958	ISOLATION PEAK 1958	ALLENS PARK 1957	RAYMOND 1957
GRANBY 1957	STRAWBERRY LAKE 1958	MONARCH LAKE 1958	WARD 1957	GOLD HILL 1957

INDEX TO 7.5-MINUTE MAPS

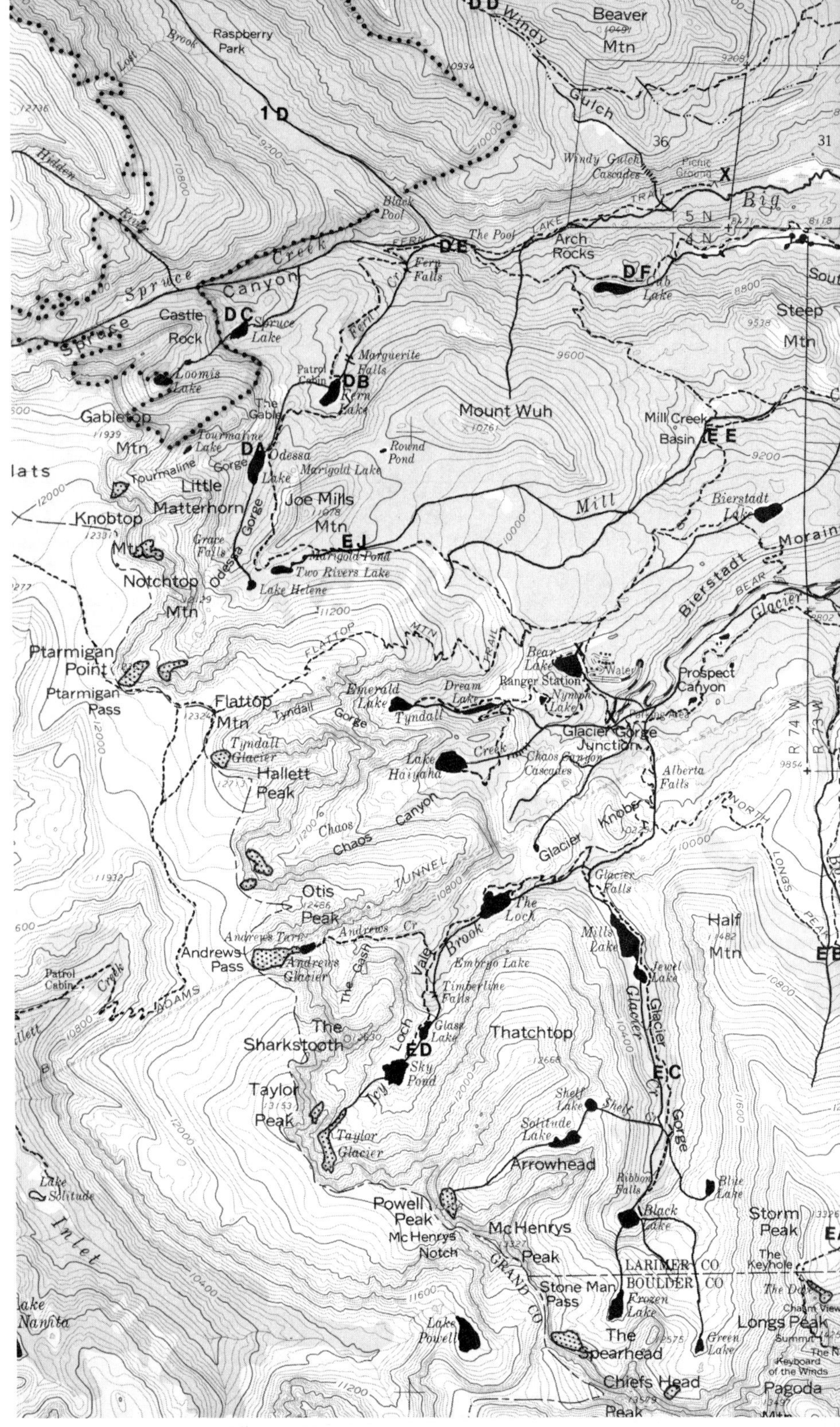

Raspberry Park
Lost Brook
D D
Windy Gulch
Beaver Mtn
1 D
Hidden River
Windy Gulch Cascades
Picnic Ground
X
36
31
Black Pool
Big
5 N
4 N
Spruce Creek
Canyon
The Pool
Fern
D E
Arch Rocks
Fern Falls
D F
Cub Lake
Steep Mtn
Castle Rock
D C
Spruce Lake
Fern Cr
Marguerite Falls
Loomis Lake
Patrol Cabin
D B
Fern Lake
Mount Wuh
Gabletop Mtn
The Gable
Tourmaline Lake
D A
Odessa Lake
Round Pond
Mill Creek Basin
E E
Tourmaline Gorge
Little Matterhorn
Marigold Lake
Knobtop Mtn
Joe Mills Mtn
Mill
Bierstadt Lake
E J
Grace Falls
Odessa Gorge
Marigold Pond
Two Rivers Lake
Moraine
Notchtop Mtn
Lake Helene
Bierstadt
Bear
Glacier
Flattop Mtn Trail
Ptarmigan Point
Ptarmigan Pass
Bear Lake
Water
Ranger Station
Nymph Lake
Prospect Canyon
Flattop Mtn
Tyndall Gorge
Emerald Lake
Dream Lake
Tyndall Creek
Glacier Gorge Junction
Tyndall Glacier
Lake Haiyaha
Chaos Canyon Cascades
Alberta Falls
R 74 W
R 73 W
Hallett Peak
Chaos Canyon
Glacier Knobs
North Longs Peak
Tunnel
Glacier Falls
Otis Peak
The Loch
Half Mtn
Mills Lake
Andrews Tarn
Andrews Cr
Andrews Pass
Andrews Glacier
The Cash
Vale Brook
Embryo Lake
Jewel Lake
E B
Patrol Cabin
Creek
Adams
Timberline Falls
Glacier
Glacier
The Sharkstooth
Loch
Glass Lake
E D
Thatchtop
Sky Pond
Taylor Peak
Icy
E C
Shelf Lake
Shelf
Solitude Lake
Cr
Gorge
Taylor Glacier
Arrowhead
Lake Solitude
Inlet
Ribbon Falls
Blue Lake
Powell Peak
Black Lake
Storm Peak
McHenrys Notch
McHenrys Peak
The Keyhole
Grand Co
Larimer Co
Boulder Co
Lake Nanita
Stone Man Pass
Frozen Lake
Lake Powell
The Spearhead
Green Lake
Longs Peak
Chiefs Head Peak
Keyboard of the Winds
Pagoda

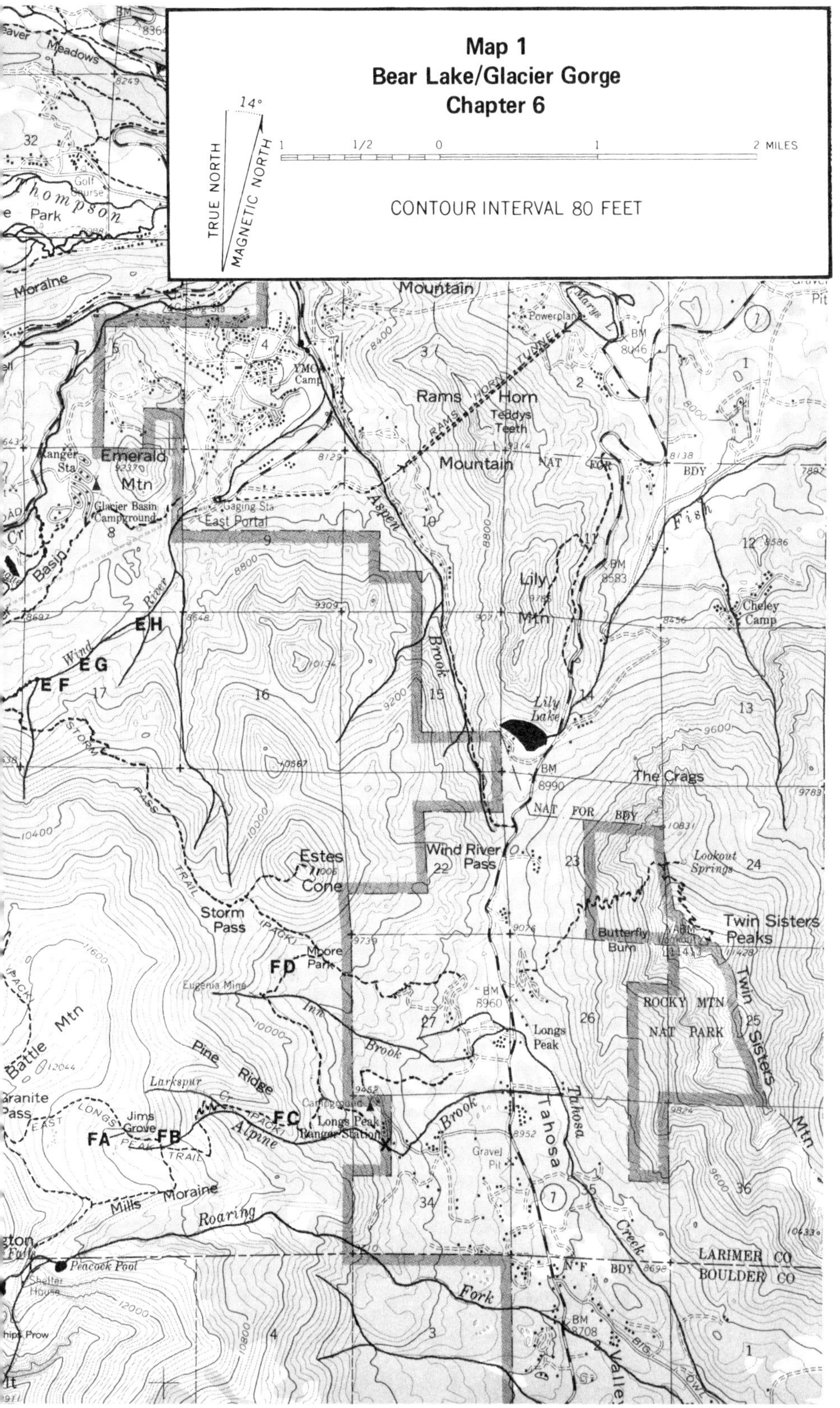
Map 1
Bear Lake/Glacier Gorge
Chapter 6
14°
TRUE NORTH
MAGNETIC NORTH
1 1/2 0 1 2 MILES
CONTOUR INTERVAL 80 FEET
Meadows
Park
Moraine
Emerald Mtn
Ranger Sta
Glacier Basin Campground
East Portal
Mountain
Powerplant
YMCA Camp
Rams Horn
Teadys Teeth
Mountain
NAT FOR BDY
Aspen
Lily Mtn
Lily Lake
Cheley Camp
Brook
Wind
River
EH
EG
EF
STORM PASS TRAIL
Estes Cone
Wind River Pass
The Crags
Lookout Springs
Twin Sisters Peaks
Butterfly Burn
Storm Pass
Moore Park
FD
Eugenia Mine
Inn Brook
Longs Peak
ROCKY MTN NAT PARK
Twin Sisters Mtn
Battle Mtn
Pine Ridge
Larkspur
Granite Pass
Jims Grove
EAST LONGS PEAK TRAIL
FA
FB
FC
Campground
Longs Peak Ranger Station
Alpine Brook
Tahosa
Mills Moraine
Roaring
Fork
Peacock Pool
Shelter House
Tahosa Creek
LARIMER CO
BOULDER CO
N F BDY
Gravel Pit

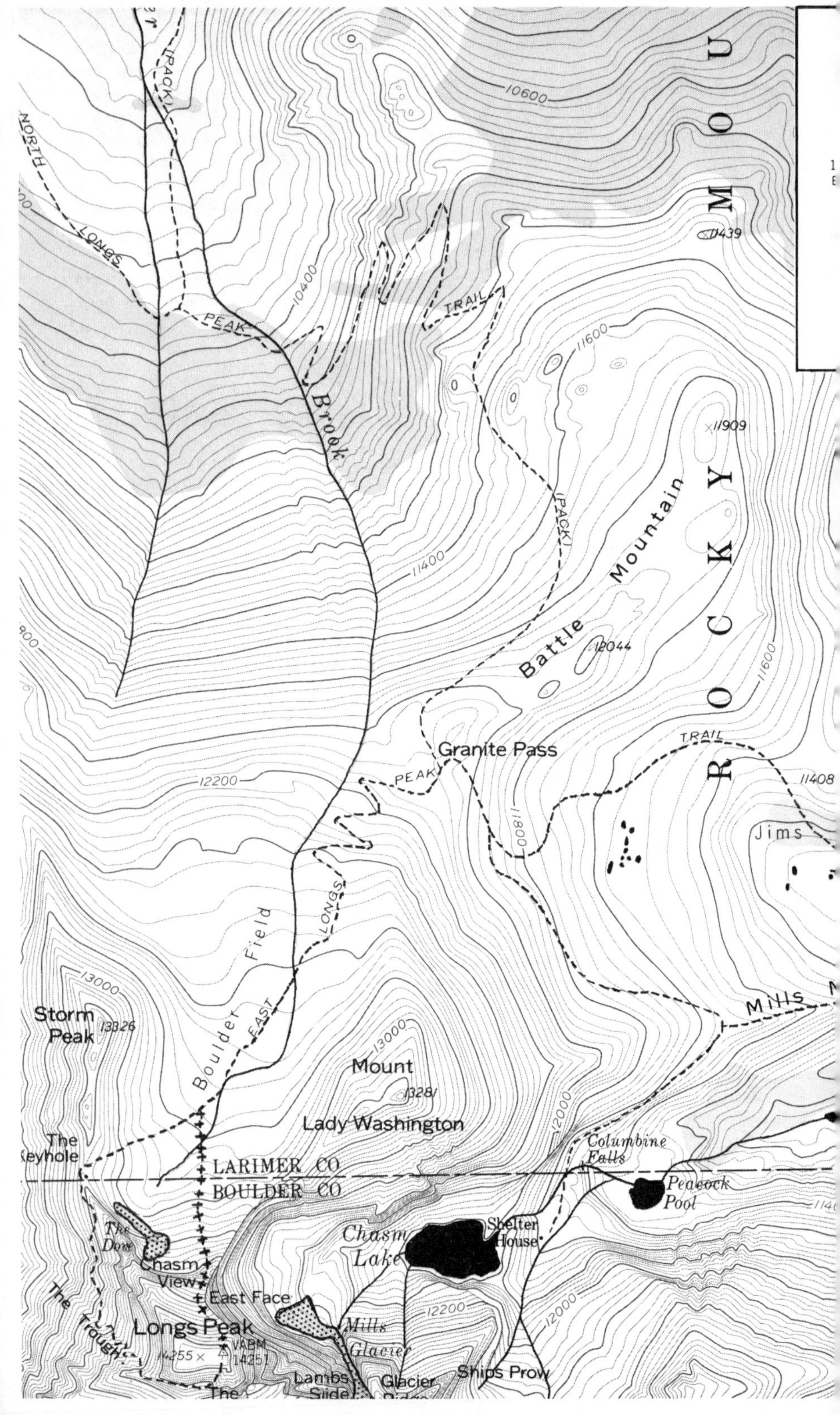

ROCKY MOU
NORTH LONGS PEAK TRAIL
(PACK)
Brook
10600
10400
11439
11600
11909
Battle Mountain
11400
12044
Granite Pass
PEAK TRAIL
12200
11800
11408
Jims
Boulder Field
LONGS
EAST
13000
Storm Peak
13326
Mount Lady Washington
13281
Mills
The Keyhole
LARIMER CO
BOULDER CO
Columbine Falls
Peacock Pool
12000
The Dove
Chasm View
Chasm Lake
Shelter House
East Face
The Trough
Longs Peak
14255
VABM 14251
Mills Glacier
12200
Lambs Slide
Glacier Ridge
Ships Prow

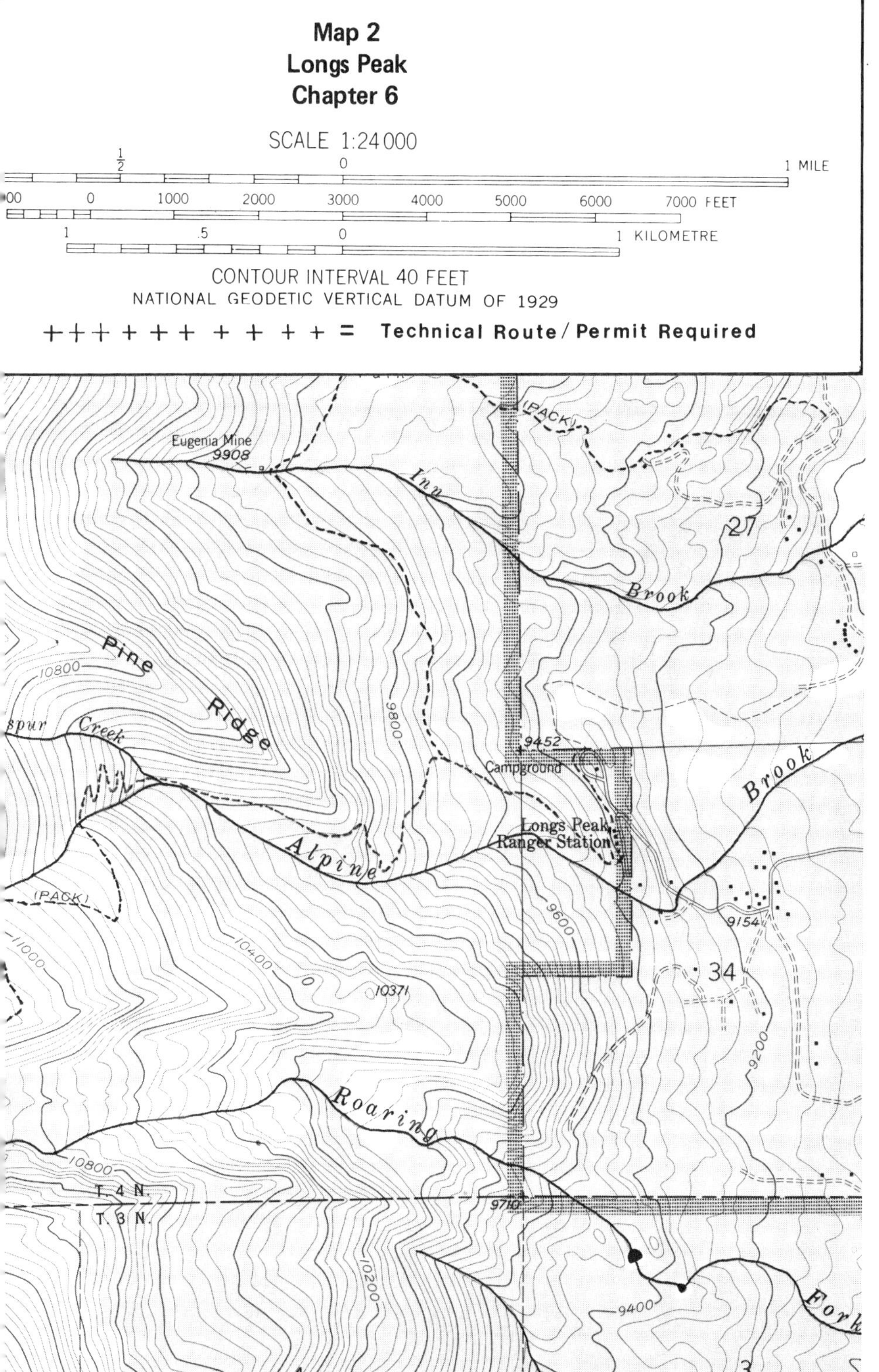

Map 2
Longs Peak
Chapter 6
SCALE 1:24 000
1/2
0
1 MILE
0
1000
2000
3000
4000
5000
6000
7000 FEET
1
.5
0
1 KILOMETRE
CONTOUR INTERVAL 40 FEET
NATIONAL GEODETIC VERTICAL DATUM OF 1929
+++ + ++ + + + + = Technical Route / Permit Required
(PACK)
Eugenia Mine
9908
Inn
27
Brook
Pine
10800
Ridge
spur
Creek
9800
9452
Campground
Brook
Longs Peak
Ranger Station
Alpine
(PACK)
9600
9154
11000
10400
10371
34
9200
Roaring
10800
T. 4 N.
T. 3 N.
9710
10200
9400
Fork
4
3

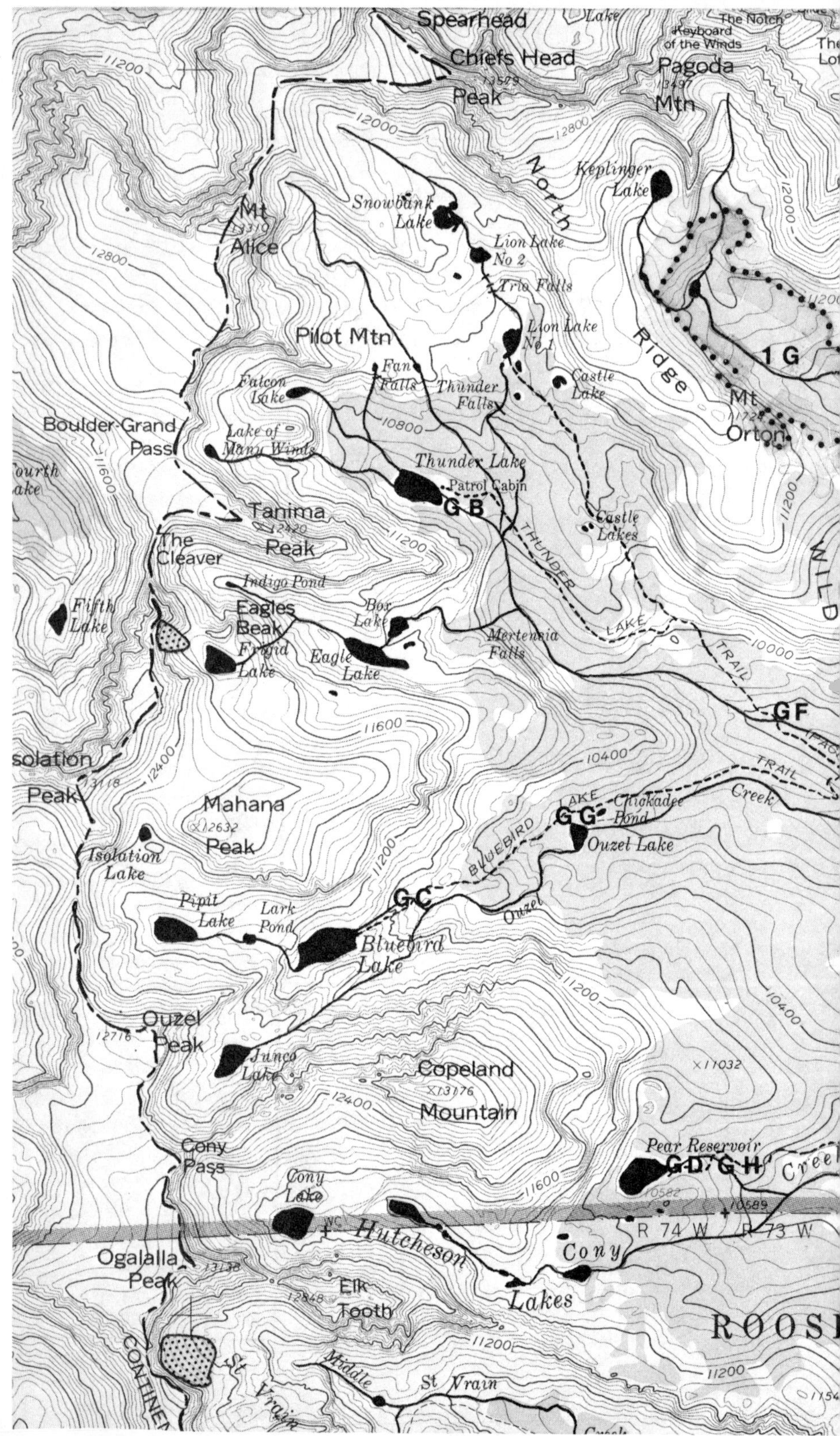

Spearhead
Chiefs Head
Peak
13579
The Notch
Keyboard of the Winds
Pagoda
Mtn
13497
North
Ridge
Keplinger Lake
Snowbank Lake
Lion Lake No 2
Trio Falls
Lion Lake No 1
Mt Alice
13310
Pilot Mtn
Fan Falls
Falcon Lake
Thunder Falls
Castle Lake
Boulder-Grand Pass
Lake of Many Winds
Thunder Lake
Patrol Cabin
GB
1G
Mt Orton
11724
Tanima Peak
12420
The Cleaver
Castle Lakes
THUNDER LAKE TRAIL
Indigo Pond
Fifth Lake
Eagles Beak
Box Lake
Frigid Lake
Eagle Lake
Mertensia Falls
GF
Isolation Peak
13118
Mahana Peak
12632
Isolation Lake
BLUEBIRD LAKE TRAIL
Chickadee Pond
GG
Ouzel Lake
Creek
GC
Ouzel
Pipit Lake
Lark Pond
Bluebird Lake
Ouzel Peak
12716
Junco Lake
Copeland Mountain
13176
11032
Cony Pass
Cony Lake
Pear Reservoir
GD GH
Creek
10582
10589
R 74 W
R 73 W
Hutcheson
Cony
Lakes
Ogalalla Peak
13138
Elk Tooth
12848
ROOS
CONTINEN
Middle St Vrain

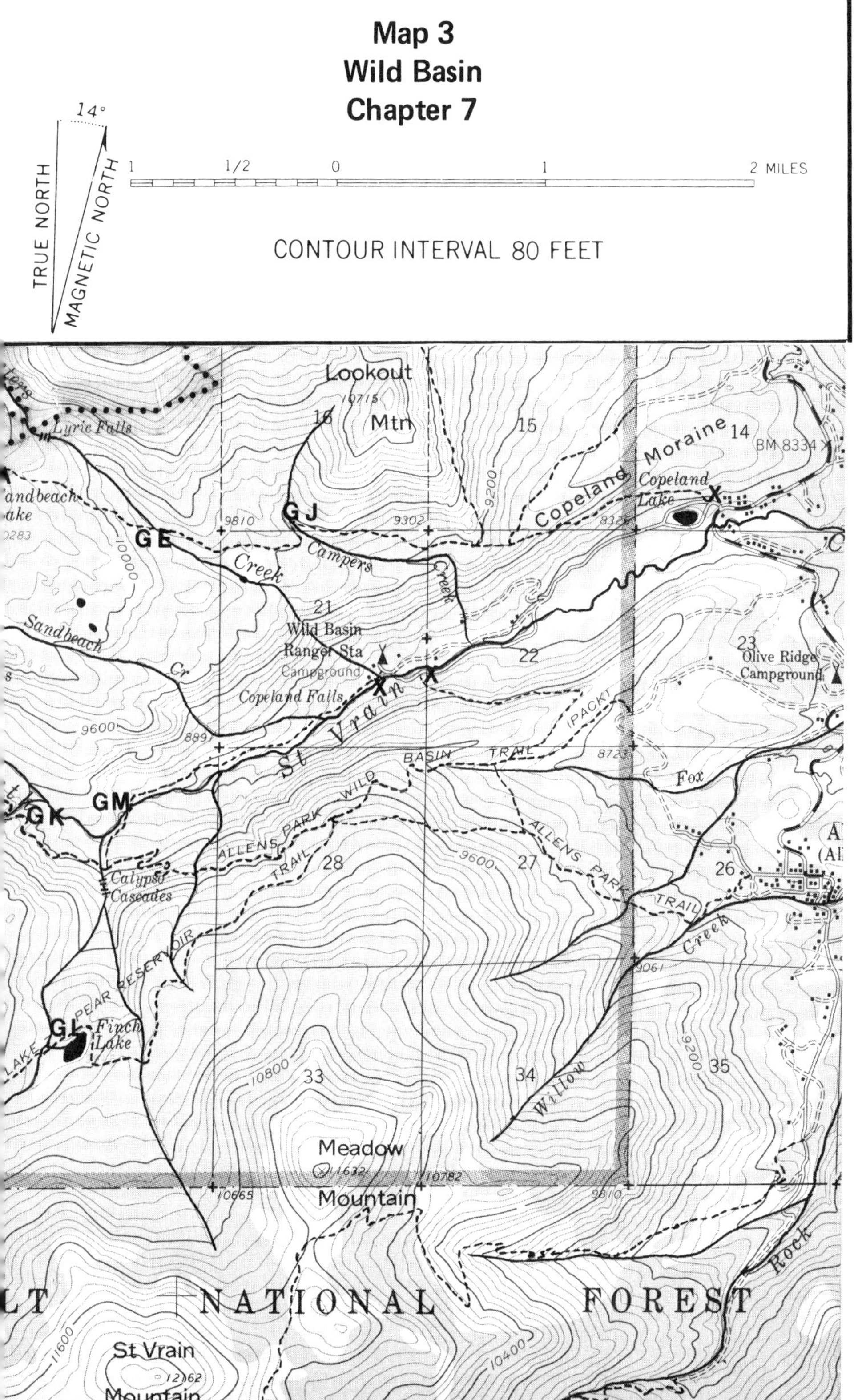
Map 3
Wild Basin
Chapter 7
14°
TRUE NORTH
MAGNETIC NORTH
1 1/2 0 1 2 MILES
CONTOUR INTERVAL 80 FEET
Lookout
Mtn
10715
16
15
14
BM 8334
Lyric Falls
Copeland Moraine
Copeland
Lake
GJ
GE
9810
9302
8328
9200
Campers
Creek
21
Wild Basin
Ranger Sta
Campground
Copeland Falls
22
23
Olive Ridge
Campground
Sandbeach
Cr
9600
8723
(PACK)
BASIN TRAIL
WILD
St Vrain
GK
GM
ALLENS PARK
TRAIL
28
27
26
9600
ALLENS PARK
TRAIL
Fox
Creek
Calypso
Cascades
PEAR RESERVOIR
LAKE
GL
Finch
Lake
9061
33
34
35
10800
9200
Willow
Meadow
Mountain
11632
10782
10665
9810
Rock
NATIONAL FOREST
St Vrain
Mountain
12162
11600
10400

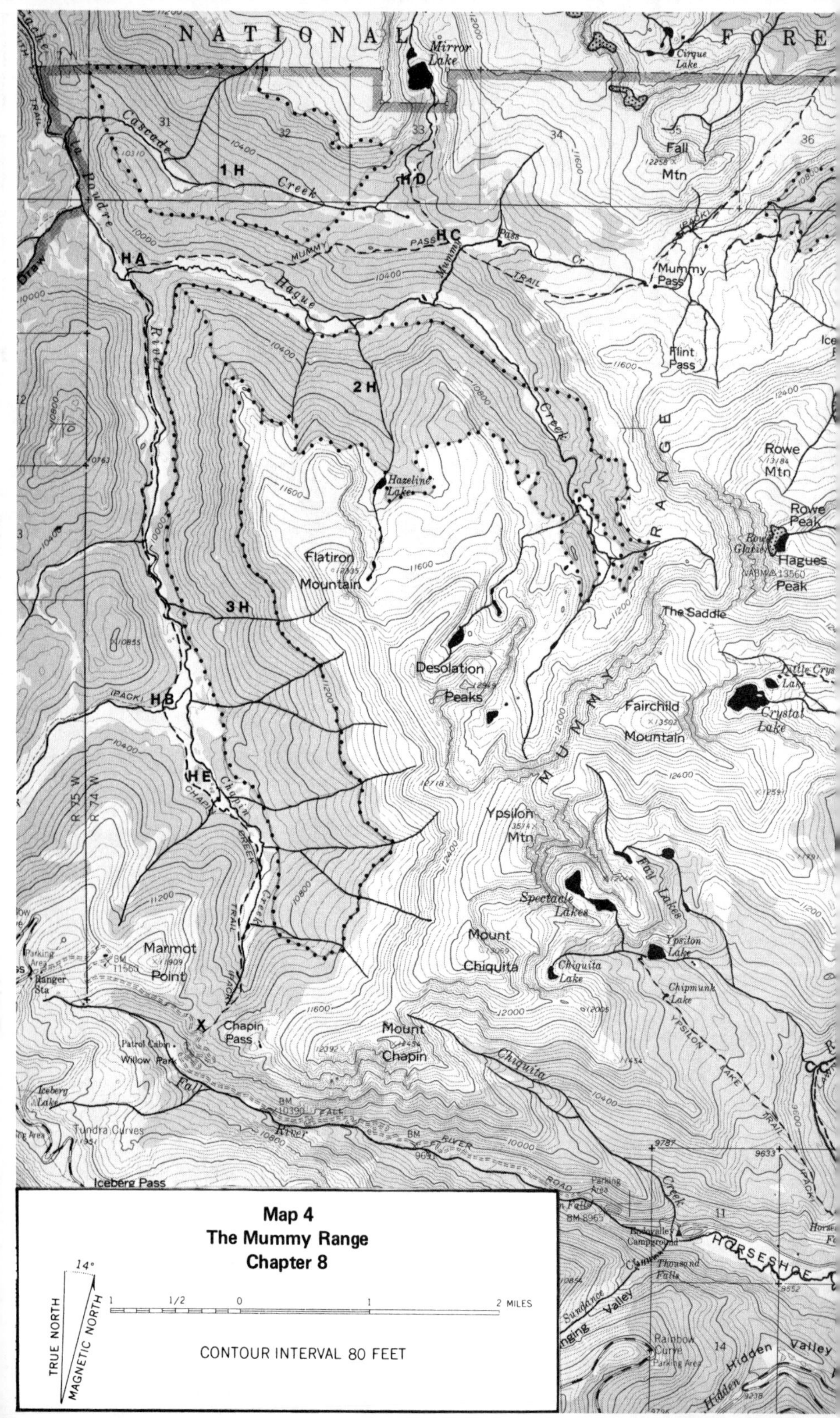
NATIONAL FORE
Mirror Lake
Cirque Lake
Cascade Creek
1 H
HD
HC
HA
HB
HE
2 H
3 H
X
Mummy Pass Trail
Fall Mtn
Mummy Pass
Flint Pass
Hague Creek
La Poudre River
Hazeline Lake
Flatiron Mountain
Desolation Peaks
MUMMY RANGE
Rowe Mtn
Rowe Peak
Rowe Glacier
Hagues Peak
The Saddle
Fairchild Mountain
Crystal Lake
Little Crystal Lake
Ypsilon Mtn
Spectacle Lakes
Fay Lakes
Ypsilon Lake
Chipmunk Lake
Mount Chiquita
Chiquita Lake
Chapin Creek
Chapin Pass
Marmot Point
Mount Chapin
Ranger Sta
Patrol Cabin
Willow Park
Iceberg Lake
Tundra Curves
Iceberg Pass
Fall River Road
Ypsilon Lake Trail
Chiquita Creek
Endovalley Campground
Horseshoe
Thousand Falls
Sundance
Hanging Valley
Rainbow Curve Parking Area
Hidden Valley
R 75 W
R 74 W
Map 4
The Mummy Range
Chapter 8
14°
TRUE NORTH
MAGNETIC NORTH
1 1/2 0 1 2 MILES
CONTOUR INTERVAL 80 FEET

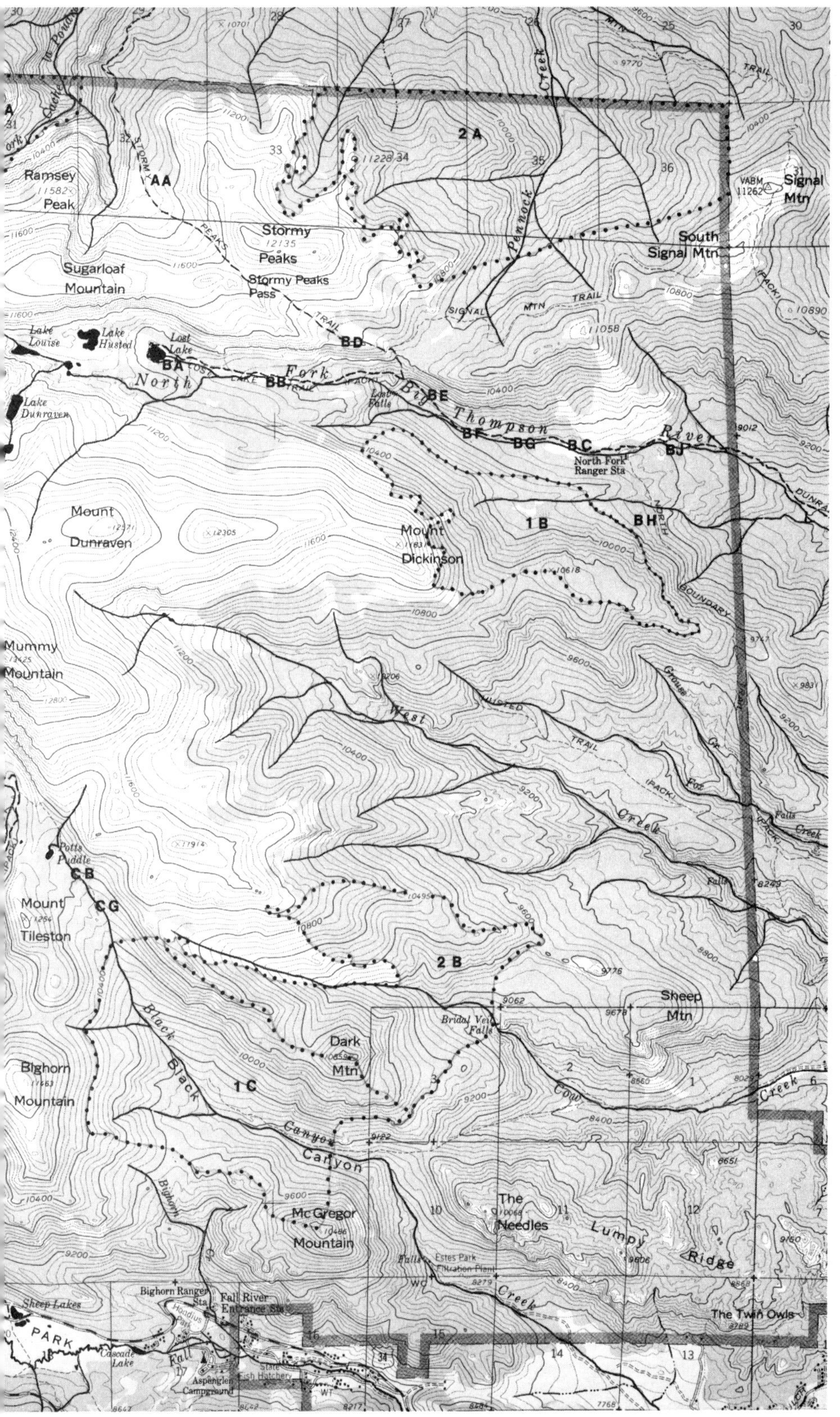

Ramsey Peak
Sugarloaf Mountain
Stormy Peaks
Stormy Peaks Pass
AA
2 A
Signal Mtn
South Signal Mtn
SIGNAL MTN TRAIL
Pennock Creek
Lake Louise
Lake Husted
Lost Lake
Lake Dunraven
BA
BB
BD
BE
BF
BG
BC
BJ
BH
North Fork Big Thompson River
Lost Falls
North Fork Ranger Sta
Mount Dunraven
Mount Dickinson
1 B
Mummy Mountain
West
HUSTED TRAIL
Grouse Cr
Fox Creek
Falls Creek
Potts Puddle
CB
CG
Mount Tileston
2 B
Sheep Mtn
Bridal Veil Falls
Dark Mtn
Black Canyon Creek
1 C
Bighorn Mountain
McGregor Mountain
The Needles
Lumpy Ridge
Cow Creek
Estes Park Filtration Plant
The Twin Owls
Sheep Lakes
Bighorn Ranger Sta
Fall River Entrance Sta
PARK
Cascade Lake
Aspenglen Campground
State Fish Hatchery

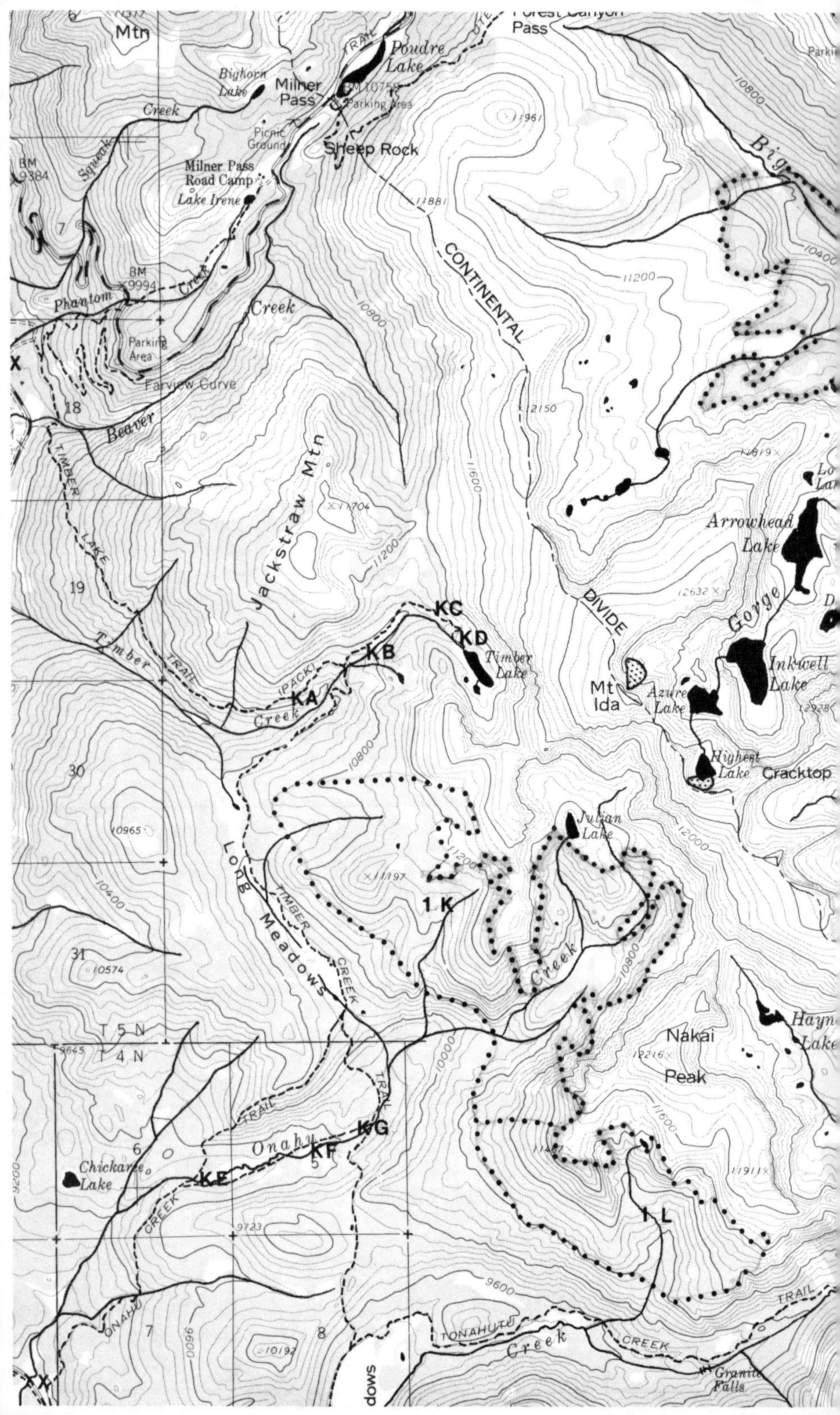

Forest Canyon Pass
Mtn
Poudre Lake
Bighorn Lake
Milner Pass
BM 10758
Parking Area
Creek
Picnic Ground
Sheep Rock
BM 9384
Squeak
Milner Pass Road Camp
Lake Irene
11961
11881
10800
Big
10400
CONTINENTAL
11200
BM 9994
Phantom
Creek
Creek
10800
Parking Area
Farview Curve
Beaver
18
TIMBER
Jackstraw Mtn
12150
11600
11819
Arrowhead Lake
11704
11200
LAKE
19
12632
DIVIDE
Gorge
KC
KD
Timber Lake
KB
Timber
TRAIL
PACK
KA
Creek
Mt Ida
Azure Lake
Inkwell Lake
12928
10800
30
Highest Lake
Cracktop
Julian Lake
10965
Long Meadows
11200
11197
12000
1 K
TIMBER
10400
CREEK
Creek
10800
31
10574
T 5 N
T 4 N
9645
10000
TRAIL
Nakai Peak
12216
Hayn Lake
TRAIL
KG
11600
6
Onahu
KF
5
11467
Chickaree Lake
KE
CREEK
11911
9200
1 L
9723
9600
ONAHU
TRAIL
7
9600
8
TONAHUTU
Creek
CREEK
10192
Granite Falls
dows
X

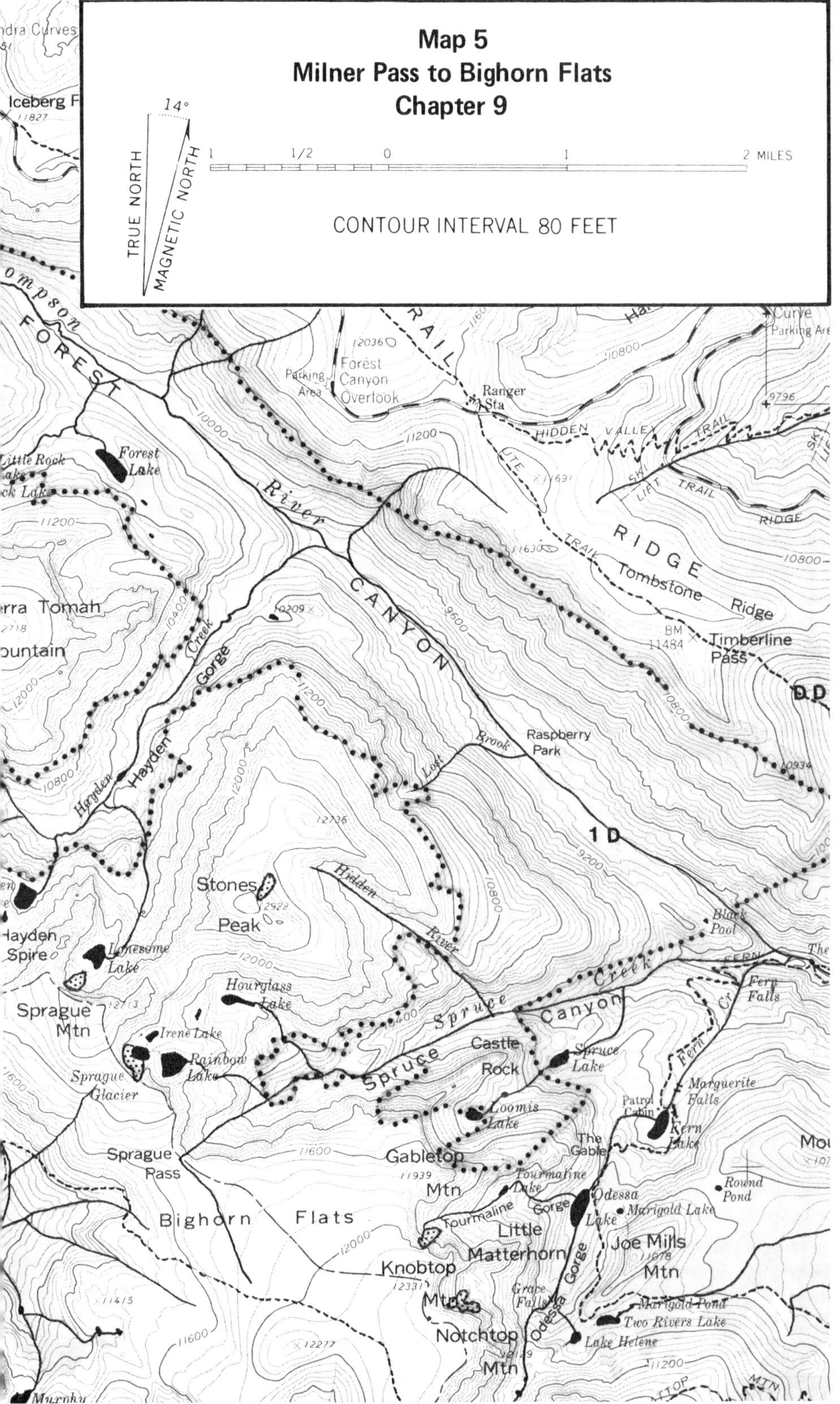
Map 5
Milner Pass to Bighorn Flats
Chapter 9
14°
TRUE NORTH
MAGNETIC NORTH
1 1/2 0 1 2 MILES
CONTOUR INTERVAL 80 FEET
Iceberg
Forest Lake
Forest Canyon Overlook
Parking Area
Ranger Sta
HIDDEN VALLEY
TRAIL
SKI LIFT TRAIL
RIDGE
Tombstone Ridge
Timberline Pass
BM 11484
FOREST
River
CANYON
Raspberry Park
Lost Brook
1 D
Hayden Gorge
Hayden Creek
Hayden Spire
Lonesome Lake
Sprague Mtn
Sprague Glacier
Stones Peak
Hidden River
Hourglass Lake
Irene Lake
Rainbow Lake
Spruce Creek
Spruce Canyon
Castle Rock
Spruce Lake
Loomis Lake
Gabletop Mtn
Black Pool
Fern Falls
Fern Cr
Marguerite Falls
Patrol Cabin
Fern Lake
The Gable
Round Pond
Tourmaline Lake
Tourmaline Gorge
Odessa Lake
Marigold Lake
Little Matterhorn
Joe Mills Mtn
Sprague Pass
Bighorn Flats
Knobtop Mtn
Grace Falls
Odessa Gorge
Marigold Pond
Two Rivers Lake
Notchtop Mtn
Lake Helene

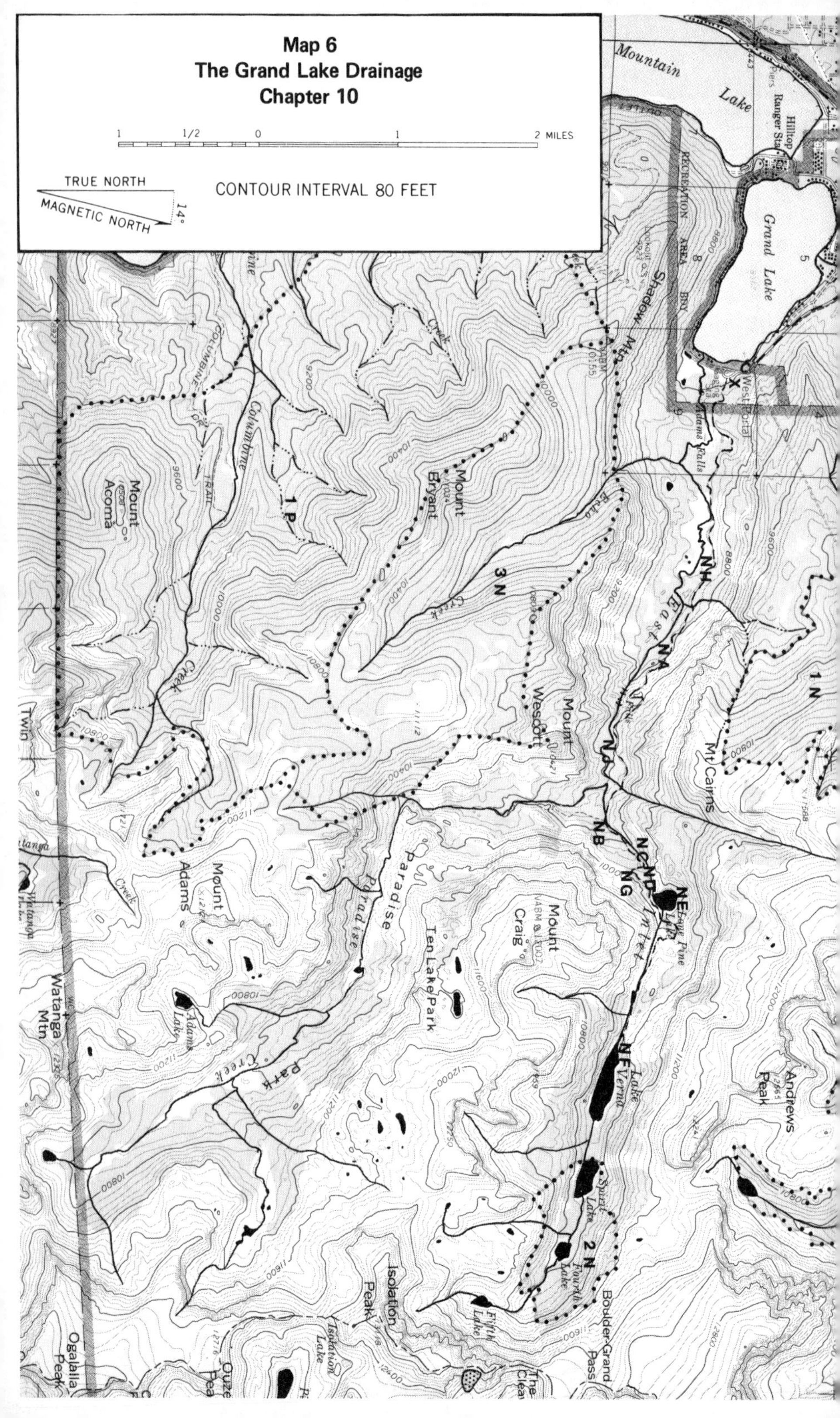

Map 6
The Grand Lake Drainage
Chapter 10
1 1/2 0 1 2 MILES
TRUE NORTH
MAGNETIC NORTH
14°
CONTOUR INTERVAL 80 FEET
Mountain Lake
Grand Lake
Shadow Mtn
West Portal
Adams Falls
Mount Acoma
Mount Bryant
Columbine Creek
Mount Wescott
Mt Cairns
East Inlet
Mount Adams
Paradise Creek
Ten Lake Park
Mount Craig
Lone Pine Lake
Verna Lake
Spirit Lake
Fourth Lake
Fifth Lake
Andrews Peak
Isolation Peak
Watanga Mtn
Ogalalla Peak
Boulder-Grand Pass
Adams Lake
Park Creek
1 P
3 N
1 N
2 N
NA
NB
NC
ND
NE
NF
NG
NH

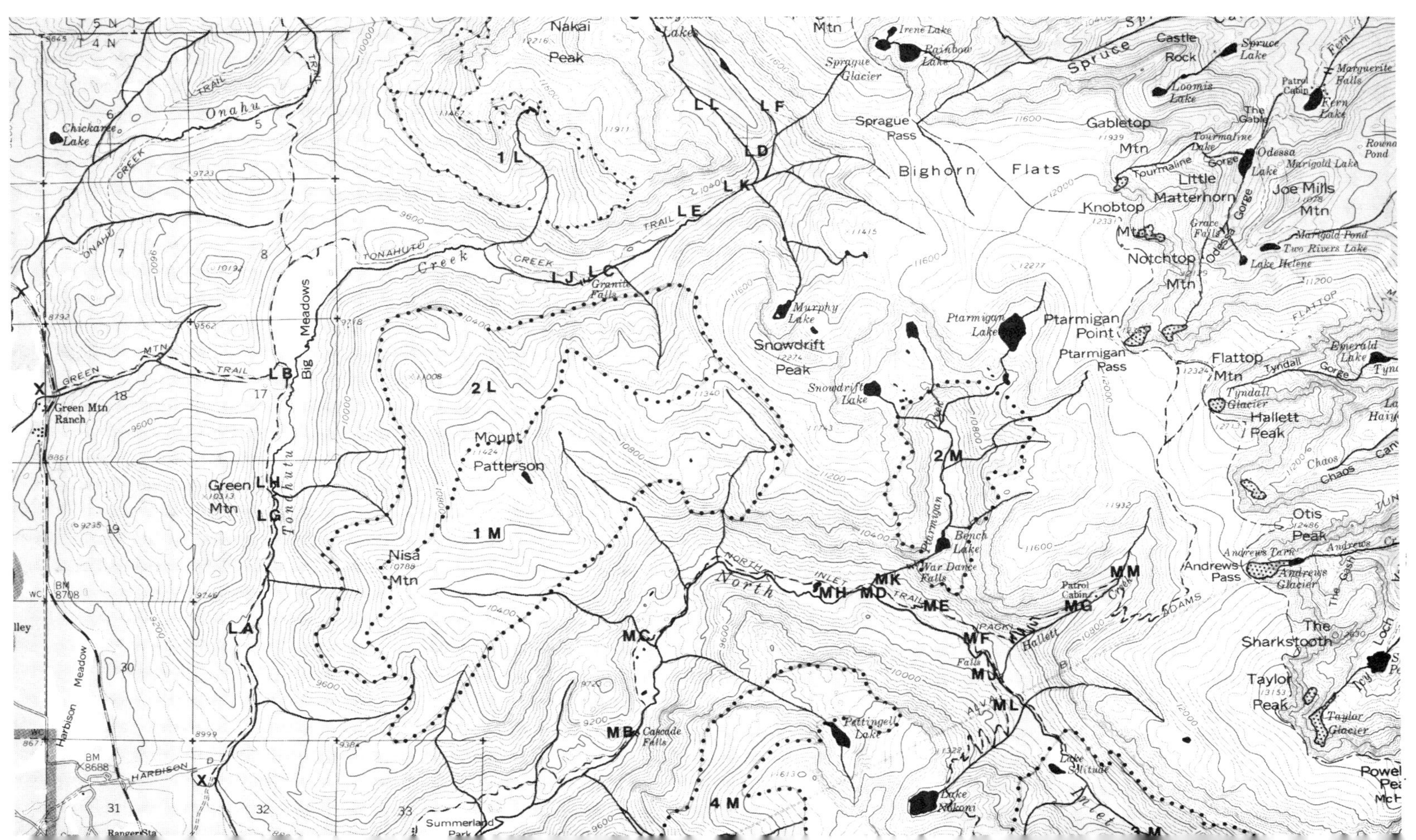

T 5 N
T 4 N
Chickaree Lake
Onahu
ONAHU CREEK
TRAIL
Nakai Peak
1 L
LL
LF
LD
LK
LE
TRAIL
TONAHUTU Creek
CREEK
LJ
LC
Granite Falls
Irene Lake
Rainbow Lake
Sprague Glacier
Sprague Pass
Bighorn Flats
Spruce
Castle Rock
Spruce Lake
Loomis Lake
Patrol Cabin
Fern Lake
Marguerite Falls
The Gable
Gabletop Mtn
Tourmaline Lake
Tourmaline Gorge
Odessa Lake
Marigold Lake
Rowena Pond
Little Matterhorn
Joe Mills Mtn
Knobtop Mtn
Grace Falls
Odessa Gorge
Marigold Pond
Two Rivers Lake
Lake Helene
Notchtop Mtn
FLATTOP
Big Meadows
GREEN MTN TRAIL
LB
Green Mtn Ranch
Murphy Lake
Snowdrift Peak
Ptarmigan Lake
Ptarmigan Point
Ptarmigan Pass
Flattop Mtn
Tyndall Gorge
Emerald Lake
Tyndall Glacier
Hallett Peak
Snowdrift Lake
2 L
Mount Patterson
2 M
Ptarmigan Creek
Green Mtn
LH
LG
Tonahutu
1 M
Nisa Mtn
Bench Lake
War Dance Falls
Chaos
Chaos Canyon
Otis Peak
Andrews Tarn
Andrews Pass
Andrews Glacier
The Gash
North Inlet
NORTH INLET TRAIL
MK
MH
MD
ME
Patrol Cabin
MM
MG
ADAMS
LA
Harbison Meadow
MC
MF
Hallett
Falls
MJ
ML
The Sharkstooth
Taylor Peak
Taylor Glacier
Icy Brook
Loch
MB
Cascade Falls
Pettingell Lake
Lake Solitude
Lake Nokoni
4 M
3 M
Inlet
HARBISON
X
Summerland Park
Ranger Sta
Powell Peak
McHenrys

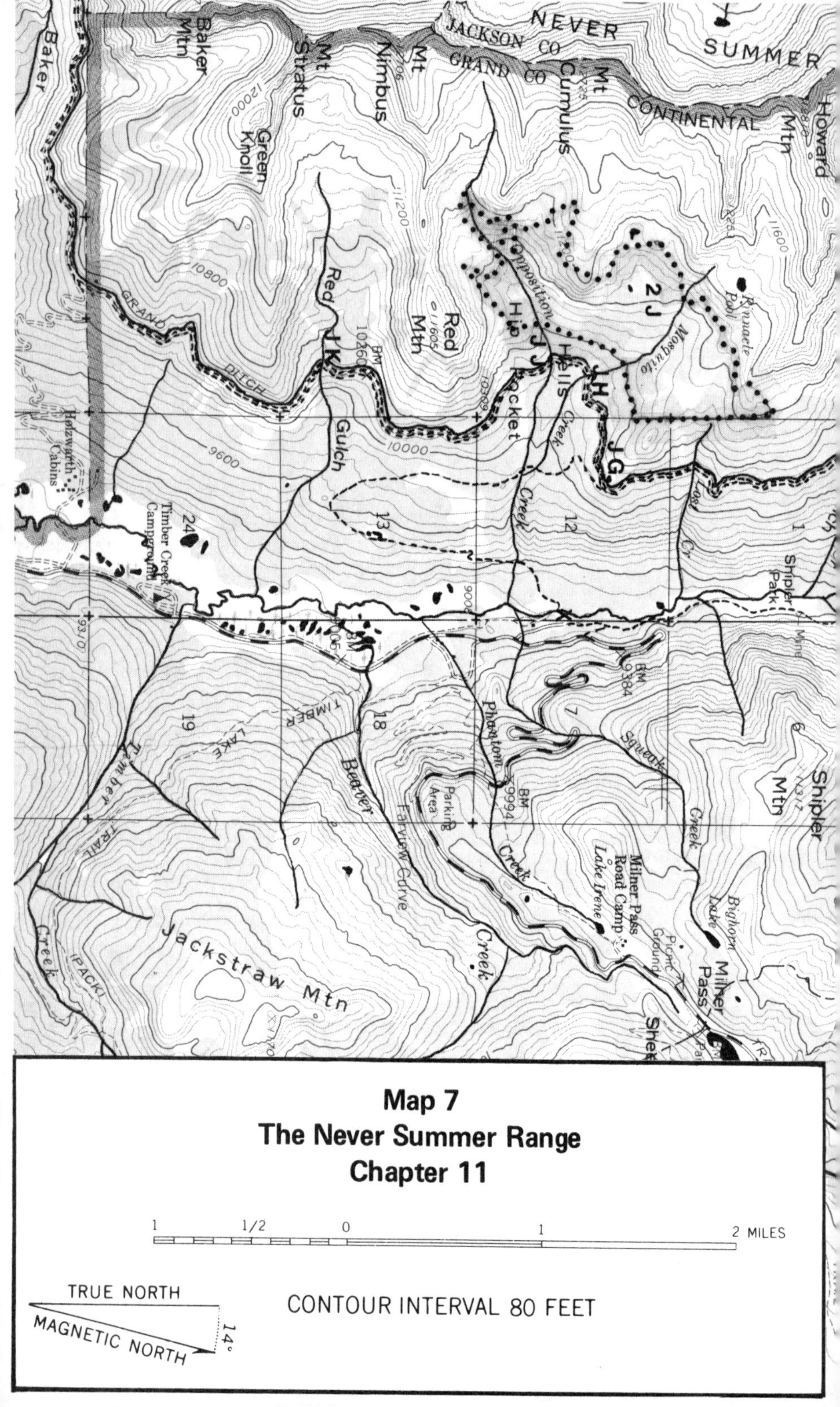

Map 7
The Never Summer Range
Chapter 11

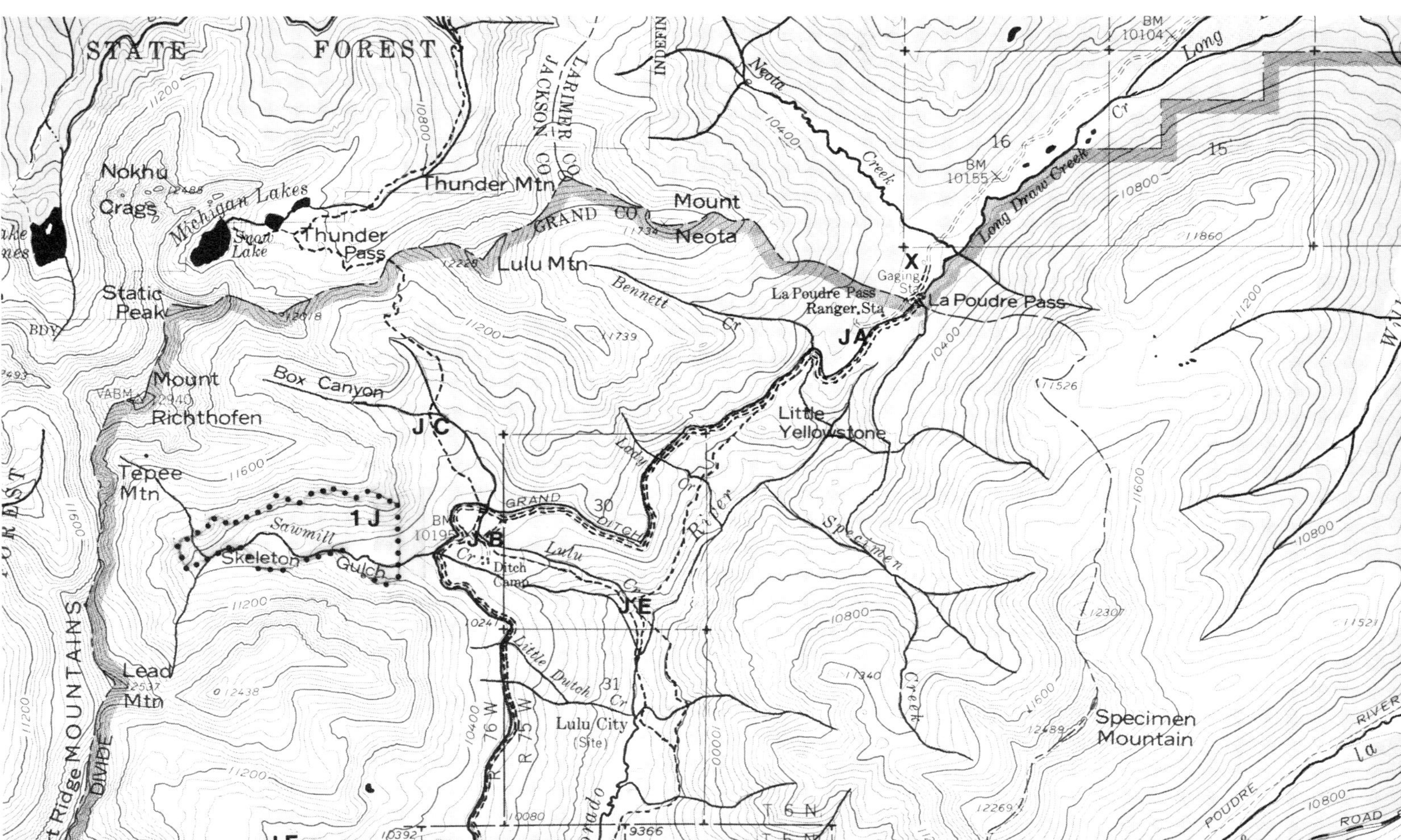

STATE
FOREST
Nokhu
Crags
Michigan Lakes
Snow
Lake
Thunder
Pass
Thunder Mtn
LARIMER CO
JACKSON CO
GRAND CO
Mount
Neota
Lulu Mtn
Static
Peak
BDY
Mount
Richthofen
VABM
Tepee
Mtn
Box Canyon
J C
1 J
Sawmill
Skeleton
Gulch
J B
Ditch
Camp
GRAND
DITCH
Lulu
Cr
J E
Little
Dutch
Cr
Lulu City
(Site)
Lead
Mtn
Ridge MOUNTAINS
DIVIDE
R 76 W
R 75 W
T 6 N
Bennett
Cr
Lady
Cr
River
Little
Yellowstone
Specimen
Creek
Specimen
Mountain
La Poudre Pass
Ranger Sta
La Poudre Pass
J A
X
Gaging
Sta
Neota
Creek
Long Draw Creek
Long
Cr
BM
10155
BM
10104
BM
10195
16
15
30
31
POUDRE
RIVER
ROAD
INDEFIN

Chapter 6

Bear Lake, Glacier Gorge, and Longs Peak

BEAR LAKE ROAD

From Glacier Basin campground, elevation 8,600 feet, to:

DESTINATION	MILEAGE	ELEVATION (ft.)
Glacier Gorge junction	3.8	9,240
Storm Pass trail junction	1.5	
From Bierstadt Lake trailhead to:		
Bierstadt Lake	1.5	9,416
From Hallowell Park to:		
Mill Creek Basin	1.5	9,000

MORAINE PARK AREA

From Fern Lake trailhead, elevation 8,150 feet, to:

DESTINATION	MILEAGE	ELEVATION (ft.)
Cub Lake	3.0	8,600
Fern Falls	2.8	8,800
Fern Lake	3.8	9,520
Mill Creek Basin	4.0	9,000
Mill Creek/Cub Lake trail junction	2.5	8,640
Odessa Lake	4.3	10,000
Spruce Lake	4.5	9,640
The Pool	1.8	8,280
From Cub Lake trailhead to:		
Cub Lake	2.5	8,600

BEAR LAKE AREA

From Bear Lake, elevation 9,440 feet, to:

DESTINATION	MILEAGE	ELEVATION (ft.)
Bear Lake nature trail	0.5	9,440
Bierstadt Lake cutoff	1.3	9,700
Bierstadt Lake	2.0	9,416
Dream Lake	1.0	9,880
Dream Lake Overlook	1.5	10,400
Emerald Lake	1.8	10,080
Emerald Lake Overlook	3.0	11,280
Fern Lake	4.8	9,520
Flattop Mountain trail junction	1.0	9,960
Flattop Mountain	4.5	12,324
Lake Haiyaha	2.3	10,200
Lake Helene spur	3.0	10,600
Loch-Mills trail junction	2.0	9,780
Mill Creek Basin	2.3	9,000
Nymph Lake	0.5	9,680
Odessa Lake	4.0	10,000
Two Rivers Lake spur	2.8	10,650

BEAR LAKE AREA

It is appropriate that the description of trails in this book should begin with the area served by the trailheads at Bear Lake, Glacier Gorge Junction, and Longs Peak ranger station. These trails are some of the park's most popular and scenic. There are more lakes in this area of the park than in any other region, and consequently, a more elaborate network of trails. It wasn't many years ago that this south-central area of the park was the location of many old hotels, catering to their guests in true rustic style. Among them were Spragues Lodge at Spragues Lake, Bear Lake Lodge, Forest Canyon Inn near The Pool, and Steads Ranch in Moraine Park. These hotels now exist only in the history of Rocky Mountain National Park.

BEAR LAKE TO EMERALD LAKE

Bear Lake is reached by traveling into the park via the Bear Lake Road, on the left shortly after passing through the Beaver Meadows entrance. Three of the most popular spots, and a fine beginners hike, is the Nymph-Dream-Emerald Lake trail. From Bear Lake, hike south a short distance to the sign indicating the trail to Nymph Lake, and then proceed 0.5 mile west. Skirting the lake on the north, the trail proceeds another half mile or so up a gentle incline to Dream Lake. Dream Lake is a popular mountain vista for photographers, with Hallett Peak (which looks like the Rock of Gibraltar) as a backdrop. Emerald Lake is slightly more than another half-mile farther up the trail. At the top of this valley, formed by the massive face of Hallett Peak and the south face of Flattop Mountain, is Tyndall Glacier. There is a fine example of a *rock glacier* just before you reach Tyndall Glacier. A rock glacier is a mass of ice enclosed in boulders, such that the whole mass moves as a normal ice glacier. Due to the steepness of Tyndall Glacier, it is dangerous to travel on without an ice ax and a lot of experience.

BEAR LAKE/LAKE HAIYAHA

Lake Haiyaha is normally reached by hiking to Dream Lake and then taking the left fork (instead of going right to Emerald Lake). This involves hiking up the ridge that descends from Hallett Peak. The hike is somewhat steep at first, but soon levels, later dropping to Chaos Canyon, the next valley south. Lake Haiyaha is about one mile from Dream Lake.

From Lake Haiyaha, the trail continues on about two miles to the junction of the trails to Loch Vale and Mills Lake. This is a rather recent trail, and is not yet on the USGS maps. Taking the trail to the left, toward Glacier Gorge Junction, the hiker can return to Bear Lake via this trail. A half-mile trail connects the Bear Lake and Glacier Gorge Junction trailheads. There will be more detail about the trails beginning at Glacier Gorge Junction later in this chapter.

BIERSTADT LAKE

Bierstadt Lake can be reached either from Bear Lake or from its own trailhead on the Bear Lake Road. This is a popular hike for the novice. Bierstadt Lake is situated on the flat expanse of Bierstadt Moraine, about 2.0 miles from Bear Lake and just under 1.5 miles from the trailhead on the Bear Lake Road.*

*A *moraine* is an accumulation of earth and stones carried and eventually deposited by a glacier.

BEAR LAKE/ODESSA GORGE/FERN LAKE TRAIL

The trail leading northward to Odessa Gorge also begins at Bear Lake. Skirt the lake on the east side (on part of the 0.6-mile nature trail) and cut to your right into an aspen grove. After about 0.5 mile, you will reach the first switchback and the cutoff to Bierstadt Lake. Turn left and proceed to another fork in the trail, another 0.5 mile. Take the right fork, which goes through alternating trees and meadows to the top of Odessa Gorge and three small lakes. The first, Marigold Pond, comes into view on the left side of the trail (where there is a campsite by the same name), followed shortly by Two Rivers Lake and Lake Helene. These lakes are roughly 3.0 miles from the trailhead at Bear Lake.

Just past Two Rivers Lake, the trail takes a sharp right turn and drops into Odessa Gorge. The view is quite remarkable from this point. Notchtop Mountain can be seen at the head of the valley; and The Little Matterhorn is visible across the gorge, although from this angle, it appears to be a rocky ridge coming down from Notchtop Mountain. The trail descends to Odessa Lake, which can be seen most of the way down. When this trail connects with the Odessa Lake trail, go left a short distance to the lake. This is a fine place to camp (DA), and what appeared as a rocky ridge from above now definitely resembles the famous Matterhorn.

Fern Lake, about a half-mile below Odessa Lake, is one of the most popular camping areas (DB). The remnants of Fern Lake Lodge, which sat on the south shore for many years, were taken down in 1977. Before that time, hikers could see part of the main building of the lodge sitting quietly near the shore. Its demolition was necessitated by vandalism of the old hotel. The ranger patrol cabin, however, is still there.

Fern and Odessa lakes are frequently approached by the Fern Lake trail, originating on the extreme western side of Moraine Park. The Fern Lake trailhead road is a spur off Bear Lake Road, near Moraine Park campground. This trail to Fern and Odessa passes through some gigantic boulders called the Arch Rocks. The trail proceeds along the Big Thompson River until it crosses a bridge at The Pool. The trail rises up a short distance from the river and then levels again in a stand of spruce. The Pool campsite (DE) is on your right. This is a very easy site to reach from the Fern Lake trailhead, since it is only 1.7 miles with a rise in elevation of only about 250 feet.

Above this spot another mile is Fern Falls. Not many hikers pass these falls without stopping for pictures and a cool drink. Slightly more than one more mile brings you to Fern Lake. The trip from Bear Lake to the Fern Lake trailhead is a popular hike, about 8.5 miles one-way, mostly downhill. It is best to travel in two vehicles, leaving one at Fern Lake trailhead and driving the other to Bear Lake (though this requires more than one person in your hiking party). This same method is frequently used by cross-country skiers in winter.

Just before the ranger station at Fern Lake is the trail to Spruce Lake, location of campsite DC. This trail is about one mile in length and is poorly maintained. Longtime hikers may recognize the red blazes carved on some trees. Above Spruce Lake is Loomis Lake. Follow the creek up from the west side of Spruce Lake through dense timber. You will pass a small pond along the way, which should not be mistaken for Loomis, a short distance away. Loomis Lake is relatively remote, offers excellent fishing, and is situated below Gabletop Mountain and Castle Rock. Round trip from Fern to Loomis is about 3.0 miles. Part of the Forest Canyon cross-country zone is between Spruce and Loomis. Camping is thus allowed here, although it is not the best.

Another lake off the beaten path in the Odessa Gorge area is Tourmaline Lake. It is situated in a small valley above Odessa Lake and directly north of The Little Matterhorn. To reach it, go around the north edge of Odessa until you reach the creek from Tourmaline. Follow this drainage up, keeping to the left side. It is pretty rough bushwacking up to this little lake, but makes a fine day trip for those camped at Fern or Odessa. The round trip from Odessa is no more than 1.0 mile, but because of the grade and lack of trail it may feel like more.

CUB LAKE

Cub Lake can be reached in several ways. The most common is to start at the Cub Lake trailhead, located off the road to the Fern Lake trailhead, but about 0.8 mile earlier. From here the trail crosses the Big Thompson along the western side of Moraine Park and then goes right. A little more than a mile away are several beaver ponds. The trail takes a few switchbacks, and then levels off at Cub Lake, 2.5 miles from the start. Cub Lake was the sight of a forest fire only a few years ago, and evidence of it is plainly visible on the right side of the trail as it proceeds along the north bank.

To make a circle trip involving Cub Lake and The Pool, continue past the lake on the northwest side. Very shortly a fork is reached. To the right and almost 1.0 mile away is The Pool. You can now hike along Fern Lake trail back to Moraine Park. The round trip for the Cub Lake-Pool circle is about 5.0 miles. Cub Lake also has a campsite (DF) located on the east side of the lake.

Another alternative is to turn left at the fork after Cub Lake. This will take you to Mill Creek Basin (EE), and Bierstadt Lake, if you choose. From there you can continue on to the trailhead at Hallowell Park in the Bear Lake Road.

GLACIER GORGE/LOCH VALE AREA

From Glacier Gorge Junction, elevation 9,240 feet, to:

DESTINATION	MILEAGE	ELEVATION (ft.)
Alberta Falls	0.5	9,400
Andrews Glacier trail	3.5	10,380
Andrews Tarn	5.8	11,360
Black Lake	4.8	10,600
Boulderbrook	3.5	10,300
Boulderfield	8.5	12,800
Jewel Lake	3.0	9,920
Glass Lake	4.3	10,800
Mills Lake	2.5	9,920
Mills Lake trail junction	2.0	9,780
North Longs Peak trail junction	1.5	9,740
Shelf Lake	4.5	11,200
Sky Pond	4.5	10,880
Solitude Lake	4.8	11,400
The Loch	2.8	10,160

GLACIER GORGE AREA

This trailhead is the starting point for those trails leading into Glacier Gorge and the Loch Vale valley. The beginning

Part of the Front Range from near Glacier Basin campground. (Photograph courtesy of the National Park Service.)

of the trail takes the hiker east for a short distance and then south for about 0.5 mile to beautiful Alberta Falls. Up the trail another 0.8 mile is the fork of the Mills Lake trail and the North Longs Peak trail. Here, take the Mills Lake trail to the right. This area is another reminder of what fire can do to a forest, for there is still evidence of a burn in 1900 that destroyed hundreds of acres along the south side of Glacier Basin. One-half mile past this point is the junction of the Mills Lake and Loch Vale trails. For Mills Lake, go left a short distance, cross the bridge at Icy Brook, and begin the ascent past Glacier Falls to the lake, 0.6 mile from the Mills Lake/Loch Vale trail junction. The distance from the parking lot to this point is 2.5 miles. Mills Lake is another of those classic scenes photographed by untold thousands through the years.

Mills Lake is at the beginning of Glacier Gorge. Immediately up the trail from Mills is Jewel Lake. The trail follows Glacier Creek from here through thick, aromatic spruce trees for slightly more than 0.5 mile to Glacier Gorge campsites (EC). They are situated between Jewel Lake and a beautiful clearing with a magnificent view of the mountains of upper Glacier Gorge: Chiefs Head Peak, Pagoda Mountain, and The Spearhead. Black Lake, 0.7 mile further up, is the principal lake of the upper Gorge area. There is a small rock shelf to ascend near Ribbon Falls, just before Black Lake. The trail ends at Black Lake. To reach the alpine lakes and mountains above it, the best route is to follow the stream that enters Black Lake on your left (east). A short hike up takes you to a relatively level shelf at the end of the gorge. Blue Lake is just above and to your left. Continue following this same stream all the way through the tundra growth (which is occasionally quite thick) to Green Lake, situated in a magnificent cirque formed by The Spearhead on the west, Longs Peak on the east, and Pagoda and Chiefs Head mountains to the south. Frozen Lake is reached from here by skirting the massive face of The Spearhead to the north and about 0.5 mile west.

Shelf and Solitude lakes can be reached by leaving the trail to Black Lake at the site of a beautiful open meadow along the right side of the trail, about 0.5 mile above the Glacier Gorge campsites (EC). You'll know you're at the right spot when you see a particularly fine view of the mountains of the upper gorge area. Consult the map to locate the open area where Shelf Creek descends to meet Glacier Creek. At this point, cross Glacier Creek, to the right as you're headed up. A faint trail exists up the right side of Shelf Creek, but frequently you'll have to make your own way through fallen timber and occasionally slippery rocks. Shelf Lake sits on a rock shelf just below the appropriately named Solitude Lake. Powell Peak is at the end of this short but extremely rugged alpine valley. The Arrowhead is the towering rock face immediately south. Return by duplicating your route as closely as possible.

LOCH VALE

Loch Vale is an area whose beauty is equal to the grandeur of Glacier Gorge. Take the trail from Glacier Gorge Junction. But when you reach the Mills Lake trail junction, instead of going left, continue up the trail along Icy Brook, which is on your left. About 1.0 mile of easy hiking brings you to The Loch (the Scottish word for *lake*). Without trying to sound like a broken record, here is still another scene worthy of the photographer's attention.

The trail passes the lake on the north and proceeds along the stream to a fork. To the right is the trail to Andrews Glacier. At the bottom of this small glacier is Andrews Tarn, 5.7 miles from the trailhead. A *tarn* is a lake formed by the immediate runoff of glacial melting. Its milky color is due to minute particles of rock dust scraped away by the glacier. The rocky face to the north is Otis Peak, while The Sharkstooth is visible below the tarn to the south.

Taking the left fork of the trail straight up from The Loch brings you past Timberline Falls to Glass Lake (also known as Lake of Glass), with Sky Pond 0.4 mile above. You can follow cairns (rock piles) from Glass Lake to Sky Pond over rock slabs and boulders. Taylor Peak is at the head of the cirque formed by Powell Peak to the south and The Sharkstooth to the north. Taylor Glacier is the extremely steep snowfield you see directly above Sky Pond. Camping is permitted below Sky Pond at Lake of Glass campsite (ED). Total mileage to Sky Pond, elevation 10,800 feet, is 4.6 miles.

FLATTOP/HALLETT/OTIS

A mountaineering trip frequently undertaken by beginning alpinists is the Flattop/Hallett/Otis traverse. This "three-in-one" trip begins at Bear Lake. Although this traverse requires reasonably good physical conditioning, it presents no route-finding problems and no special climbing skills. Take the previously described trail toward Fern and Odessa lakes, but take the left cutoff, 1.0 mile up the trail, toward Flattop Mountain. Ascend through the forest for roughly 0.5 mile to the Dream Lake overlook. Much of Tyndall Gorge is visible from this vantage point. It is good to remember at places like this not to throw or kick rocks down the rocky couloir, or gorge, below you. One more mile of switchbacks takes you to timberline, and the gradual expanse of tundra from which Flattop derives its name. The "summit" is at 12,324 feet. It may come as a surprise to see that so much flat ground has the appearance of rugged mountains from places like Bear Lake. A trail leads to the left (south) from Flattop.

It ultimately ends up at Grand Lake via the North Inlet. Walk this trail a short distance and then strike off on your own near the top of Tyndall Gorge.

Hallett Peak is south of this point and about 400 feet higher. It is an easy walk to its summit at 12,713 feet. From Hallett, the next mountain on the agenda is Otis Peak, 12,486 feet, visible across Chaos Canyon to the south. The route across these three peaks follows the continental divide almost exactly. Descend Hallett to the top of Chaos Canyon and then walk along this precipice to the gradual western flank of Otis, and hike to the summit.

For the hardy and conditioned hiker, Taylor Peak, 13,153 feet, can be scaled in much the same fashion as Flattop/Hallett/Otis. Descend Otis by going southwest along the divide to Andrews Pass. Andrews Glacier lies directly below, to the east. Taylor Peak is more than a thousand feet higher than this point, and about 1.0 mile to the south. It's no more difficult to climb than the other three, but it will certainly require more effort. For those who want to climb as many mountains as possible, Powell Peak is readily accessible from Taylor Peak. It is 13,208 feet in elevation, and is southeast slightly over 1.0 mile, as the crow flies. Shelf and Solitude lakes are visible below, as well as a rare view of McHenrys Peak. This extended and ambitious traverse should end here. If your body hasn't told you that already, the imposing barrier of McHenrys Notch will.

The normal return for the Flattop to Otis (or Powell) traverse is down Andrews Glacier. This is where the ice ax, if you have brought one, will assist you in *glissading*, or sliding. Although this area is not particularly dangerous, stay away from the sides to avoid crevasses and loose rocks. Only slide on snow if you are sure you can stop yourself if necessary. There are rocks at the bottom of Andrews Glacier, not to mention the glacial lake. The changing condition of this or any glacier warrants year to year inquiry at the backcountry office. Return on the trail to The Loch, and then out to Glacier Gorge Junction or Bear Lake. After this trip, your car looks pretty good at the end of the trail.

Notchtop Mountain from near Lake Helene. This scene is in early spring when the snowpack is still intact. (Photograph by the author.)

NOTCHTOP/KNOBTOP/GABLETOP

Notchtop, 12,129 feet, Knobtop, 12,331 feet, and Gabletop, 11,939 feet, are the mountains overlooking Odessa Gorge. The normal route to ascend these three is once again via Flattop Mountain. But, instead of veering to the left toward Hallett Peak, go north and west along the rolling tundra to Ptarmigan Pass and Ptarmigan Point. Both of these spots, in close association at the top of Odessa Gorge, are named after the elusive alpine grouse of the same name. The ptarmigan is one of the best camouflaged creatures, blending in with its rocky habitat in summer, and changing to white in winter.

Skirting Ptarmigan Point, the route follows the divide north for about 0.5 mile to Notchtop. Unless you have experience and preparation for technical climbing, leave the descent to and ascent of the Notch at the top of the mountain to those who are. Knobtop, 12,331 feet, is directly north of here, and is an easy walk. The Little Matterhorn, visible from Knobtop, is the far tip of the jagged ridge, running east from the summit of Knobtop. If you choose this route, be extremely cautious in the descent to, as well as the traverse of, this ridge. Down the gradual north slope of Knobtop, and along the top of Tourmaline Gorge, is Gabletop, roughly four hundred feet lower than Knobtop. The approximate round trip distance from Bear Lake to Gabletop is 14.0 miles.

All along the divide, from Gabletop to Powell Peak, there are steep rocky faces on the east side of the mountains and flat rolling tundra on the west. This area is part of the "Flattop peneplain," with the area near Knobtop (Bighorn Flats) the most expansive. The geologic juxtaposition of sheer rock walls and flat ground is the result of glaciation of the surface of granite and schist rock, uplifted in the formation of the present Rockies. Trail Ridge Road is another excellent area to view the canyons formed by ice and water.

THE LITTLE MATTERHORN

Through the years, The Little Matterhorn, 11,586 feet, has been a favorite destination for many, including the author. It is particularly enjoyable to make the ascent in conjunction with an overnight stay at Fern Lake, or preferably, Odessa. The trip begins by following the creek up to Tourmaline Lake, as described. Ascend the snowfield on the far side of the lake for a short distance, and then veer left, climbing up the steep tundra to the ridge. Once at the ridge (which is higher than the summit register) proceed with all due caution eastward, going up, down, and around as necessary. The summit *register* is on the far tip of the ridge, and requires some tricky moves in several spots.* Some may elect to remain at the point just above the register. This is an interesting climb after a trip like Flattop, since it requires a certain amount of route-finding and surefootedness. However, it is recommended only for those who are used to some degree of exposure.**

PEAKS OF GLACIER GORGE

Glacier Gorge offers a few real challenges to weekend mountaineers as well. McHenrys Peak, 13,327 feet, is one of the most challenging mountains in the park, for it involves more than just a stroll on the tundra. To approach McHenrys, follow the trail to Black Lake. If you choose to make it a two-day trip, you may camp overnight at the Glacier Gorge sites. From Black Lake follow the stream on the east side up to the shelf surrounding Black Lake, and go west to the snowfield on the left side of the imposing east face of McHenrys Peak. At the top of this snowfield is Stone Man Pass, named for a rock outcropping nearby. Though the amount of snow on this mountain varies from June to September, an ice ax will probably come in handy. Make your way up to the pass by switchbacking on the snow and *talus.**** From Stone Man Pass the route is not as obvious. Begin by boulder-hopping up to where more vertical rock appears. Stay somewhat near, but not right on, the edge to your right. A bit more than halfway up you will encounter a draw, usually snow-filled, that must be crossed to reach the rocky outcroppings above and to the northwest. Here, an ice

*Many mountains in the park have metal canisters at their summits, secured to rock cairns. Within these metal tubes are lists with the names of people who have climbed the mountain that year and the date. Signing a summit register is a ritual, signifying the conclusion of the ascent.

**Exposure, in this context, refers to being in a position on a mountain where the drop-off is nearby and substantial.

***Talus refers to the rock debris at the base of a cliff.

ax will come in handy. Some hand-over-hand travel is required in the final ascent to the summit. The Arrowhead is plainly visible to the northeast, as well as an outstanding view of all the peaks surrounding Glacier Gorge.

Chiefs Head Peak, 13,579 feet, can be easily climbed by going south from Stone Man Pass and following the ridge to the top. It is slightly steep at first, but then becomes more gradual toward the summit. Another route to Chiefs Head will be discussed in chapter 7.

From Stone Man Pass, The Spearhead, 12,575 feet, appears as a sharp ridge extending north from the summit. The best route to The Spearhead is the approach from Frozen Lake. The easiest route to the top of the ridge is via the couloir on the west side of The Spearhead, and then just a bit north to the summit. It certainly isn't as difficult as it appears from below, but caution is advised near the top. Though it is exposed, it presents no technical problems.

Pagoda Mountain, 13,497 feet, can be climbed from the vicinity of Green Lake. There is a couloir below the face of Pagoda, southeast of the lake. Climbing up this couloir brings you to the ridge between Pagoda and Longs Peak, near the Keyboard of the Winds. The summit is just to the south and up about four hundred feet. This is a grueling ascent of almost two thousand feet in less than 0.8 mile. An alternative route, though equally rugged, is described in chapter 7, with Sandbeach Lake as a base camp.

Thatchtop, 12,668 feet, is normally climbed via Shelf and Solitude lakes. When approaching Solitude Lake, veer to the right and simply begin the ascent. The summit is about 0.5 mile north of Solitude. No route-finding is required, except perhaps when approaching the peak through the forest to Shelf Lake. Another route is up the north slope from the Mills Lake/Loch Vale junction. The only problem here is ascending the steep draw to the even steeper rock face on this northern side. This route is shorter and conceivably easier. But the previous route affords the hiker the opportunity of visiting the beautiful Shelf and Solitude lakes. A good way to see both routes is to make the round trip up the north slope, descending to the lakes.

Looking south from the Bear Lake area. Thatchtop is the pyramidal mountain at left-center. Powell Peak is in the higher valley in the background. (Photograph courtesy of the National Park Service.)

It should be understood that in the geographical areas described in this and other chapters, some mountains, waterfalls, and other landmarks are not mentioned. The rationale for this involves space considerations: it is simply impossible to mention every place you may want to venture.

LONGS PEAK AREA

From Longs Peak Ranger Station, elevation 9,390 feet, to:

DESTINATION	MILEAGE	ELEVATION (ft.)
Alpine Brook Bridge	2.0	10,600
Boulderfield	6.0	12,800
Chasm Lake	5.5	11,760
Chasm Lake trail junction	3.5	11,550
Estes Cone summit	2.5	11,006
Eugenia Mine	1.5	9,908
Eugenia Mine junction	0.5	9,680
Granite Pass	4.3	12,080
Jims Grove	3.0	11,000
Jims Grove trail junction	2.5	10,960
Moore Park	2.0	9,750

LONGS PEAK AND VICINITY

This section focuses on the Longs Peak area, which is important enough to be discussed separately. At 14,256 feet, Longs Peak is the highest and unquestionably the most famous mountain in the park. Whole books have been written on its history and climbing routes. The prominence of this mountain has made it a readily visible landmark, going back to the 1820 expedition of Stephen Long (for whom the mountain is named). The Arapahoe Indians called the Longs Peak-Mt. Meeker duo *Nesotaieux*, or ("the Two Guides"). The first recorded climb of Longs Peak was in 1868, when a one-armed Civil War veteran, Major John Wesley Powell, led a successful attempt via the Homestretch route from Wild Basin.* The Homestretch is the current route up the last pitch before the summit. This is probably the route that was taken by the earliest climbers, unknown Indians in search of eagles. It has since been climbed by thousands of local residents and visitors. Enos Mills, a climbing guide and an early advocate of the park's formation, is reputed to have climbed Longs Peak 297 times.

The most popular route taken in the ascent of Longs Peak is through The Keyhole, a rock formation on the northwest ridge of Longs on the saddle between it and Storm Peak. This route was formerly the main means of descent from the summit when most hikers went directly up the north face via the cable route. It was so named because from September 1925 until July 1973 two lengths of cable were attached to particularly tricky pitches to assist novice climbers with the ascent. One cable was 160 feet in length and the other, 30 feet. They were removed to bring climbers back to the idea of meeting the mountain on its own terms. The cable route is now classified as a technical climb. If you desire to climb

*Some readers may associate the name Powell with the original exploration of the Colorado River (then, the Grand River). This man was an avid explorer and a famous surveyor. The loss of his arm at the Battle of Shiloh didn't deter him from climbing Longs Peak, or from navigating the treacherous waters of the Colorado the next year, in 1869. Using wooden rafts, Powell's party was the first to float through the Grand Canyon.

Longs Peak from near the Chasm Lake shelter cabin. The sheer wall on the right, known as "The Diamond," draws some of the world's best technical rock climbers. There are less difficult technical routes on the east face toward the center of the photo. (Photograph courtesy of Tom Post.)

Longs Peak via this route or any on the east face, a technical permit must be obtained.

The ascent of Longs Peak usually begins at the Longs Peak ranger station, located on the extreme eastern side of the park. Access to this trailhead is from a road off Colorado Route 7, south of Estes Park, and is well marked as the way to Longs Peak campground and ranger station. Longs Peak can also be approached on the North Longs Peak trail, which starts at the Mills Lake trail near Glacier Gorge Junction. There is a campsite along this route at Boulder Brook (EB). The route from the ranger station is two miles shorter than the North Longs Peak trail, and is a more popular route. Those who camp the night before the climb should do so at either the Boulder Field (EA) or Jims Grove (FB). Along the East Longs Peak trail, the Goblins Forest campsite (FC) is available.

If you don't intend to spend the night on the trail, it is particularly important to get an early start. Due to the frequent afternoon thunderstorms, you should depart near sunup in order to ascend and begin your descent before these storms form. Starting at Longs Peak ranger station, the trail is reasonably gentle for 2.0 miles, ascending through the forest along Alpine Brook. After crossing the bridge over Alpine Brook at the 2.0-mile mark, the trail opens up to scrub vegetation near timberline. A bit more than 0.5 mile ahead is the junction of two trails. To the left and 3.0 miles further is Chasm Lake at the foot of the extraordinary east face of Longs. Just past Columbine Falls, which flows into Peacock Pool, and below Chasm Lake, there is a shelter cabin. This rock structure is utilized as a cache for rescue equipment; no camping is allowed.

To the right 0.3 mile is Jims Grove. This is a basin area below Mount Lady Washington and the less conspicuous Battle Mountain. The trail ascends this basin to Granite Pass, slightly over 1.0 mile away. This is the point where the North and East Longs Peak trails converge. From Granite Pass the trail proceeds up some switchbacks toward the north face of Longs and the Boulder Field, 1.7 miles away. From here the real climb begins.

The Keyhole is about 1.0 mile from the last switchback before the Boulder Field, and about 0.3 mile southwest of the point where the cable route cuts to the left. The small shelter before The Keyhole is dedicated to Agnes Vaille, who perished on Longs in 1925, after a successful winter ascent of the east face. After going through The Keyhole, you pass up and over the ledges, and proceed laterally south along the rocky west side of the mountain, with Glacier Gorge stretching out behind and below. Climbing up The Trough and over the southwest ridge to the left, you reach the south face of the section of trail known as the Narrows. Blaze marks along this section assist in route-finding. To the novice hiker, the Narrows are somewhat disturbing at first, because of the apparent exposure and the narrowness of the ledge the trail follows. From the Narrows the route veers up and to the left at the Homestretch. The summit, above this section of rock slabs, is ascended along a crack system.

The top of Longs Peak is, to say the least, remarkable. A description of the beauty of the mountains from this point would be pathetically inadequate. For many, the feeling of accomplishment will rival the view, and even for the well-seasoned mountaineer, the experience is one to savor. But, keep in mind a few things as you contemplate a trip to this mountain. The round trip from Longs Peak ranger station is around 17.0 miles via The Keyhole route, and requires not only acclimatization but reasonable conditioning as well. Keep your eyes on your hiking companions, the route, and the weather.

Mount Meeker, 13,911 feet, is the second highest in the park and sits next to Longs about 0.8 mile to the southeast. (See the Wild Basin map in map section.) The principal routes up this mountain originate in Wild Basin and at the Chasm Lake shelter cabin. The route from Wild Basin is fairly direct and clear-cut, originating at Sandbeach Lake. But instead of going all the way to Sandbeach, the hiker can approach Meeker by following the Hunters Creek drainage up the couloir on the south slope.

An alternate route is up Meeker's northeast ridge. At the Chasm Lake shelter cabin cross the creek and pick your way up through the rocks to the southeast. On reaching the ridge, the route to the summit becomes obvious. The extremely flat area between Mount Meeker and Longs Peak is called The Loft. The latter route is a much more interesting way of climbing Meeker. Walking up from Sandbeach Lake is tedious and seemingly unending.

Mount Lady Washington, 13,281 feet, and Storm Peak, 13,326 feet, can both be climbed easily from the Boulder

Field. Incidently, assuming the weather is good, the summit of Mount Lady Washington is an excellent location for viewing technical rock climbs on the east face of Longs, particularly those on "The Diamond," the sheerest part. Binoculars are necessary for a really good look.

North of Longs Peak and southeast of Sprague Lake on the Bear Lake Road are three campsites on Wind River (EF, EG, EH). A fisherman's trail exists from the East Portal above the YMCA camp to these sites. Moore Park campsite (FD) is located on the Storm Pass trail. You can reach it by taking the trail to the now defunct Eugenia Mine from the Longs Peak ranger station (1.5 miles), and then proceeding 0.5 mile further. This campsite is on the south side of Estes Cone, 11,006 feet. An easy trail up this mountain originates at Storm Pass, 0.5 mile northwest of Moore Park.

Twin Sisters, 11,428 feet, appears on the maps within its own boundaries, separated from the rest of the park. Its trailhead is on Colorado Route 7 between the guest ranches of Longs Peak Inn and Aspen Lodge. Three and one-half miles up the switchbacking trails takes you to the summit. A fire lookout tower, which for many years stood atop Twin Sisters, was removed in July 1977. This is a favorite conditioning hike for visitors staying in the Tahosa Valley area. Don't forget to bring your own water on this trail, because, for the most part, none is available along the way.

Chapter 7

Wild Basin

WILD BASIN AREA

From Wild Basin Ranger Station, elevation 8,700 feet, to:

DESTINATION	MILEAGE	ELEVATION (ft.)
Bluebird Lake	6.5	10,978
Bluebird Lake trail junction	3.0	9,550
Calypso Cascades	1.8	9,200
Chickadee Pond	5.0	10,000
Copeland Falls	0.3	8,710
Eagle Lake	8.0	10,800
Finch Lake cutoff	3.0	9,720
Finch Lake via Thunder Lake trail	5.3	9,912
Lion Lake No. 1	7.0	11,040
Lion Lake trail junction	4.8	10,090
Ouzel Falls	2.8	9,450
Ouzel Lake	5.0	10,000
Ouzel/Bluebird Lake junction	4.5	9,950
Pear Creek	7.0	10,520
Pear Reservoir	7.3	10,582
Thunder Lake	6.8	10,574
From Finch Lake trailhead to:		
Finch Lake/Wild Basin junction	2.5	9,720
Finch Lake	4.5	9,912
Pear Creek	6.3	10,520
Pear Reservoir	6.5	10,582
From Copeland Lake, elevation 8,400 feet, to:		
Campers Creek campsite	2.3	9,600
Hunters Creek campsite	3.3	9,780
Meeker Park trail junction	1.3	9,200
Park boundary	0.5	8,600
Sandbeach Lake	4.3	10,283

WILD BASIN TRAILS

Wild Basin is in the southeastern corner of Rocky Mountain National Park. It encompasses the entire upper drainage of the North Saint Vrain River and is profuse in lakes and streams. Joe Mills, the brother of Enos Mills, originally called this area the "Land of Many Waters." Like his brother, he was a vocal proponent for the park's formation. Joe Mills Mountain near Fern Lake bears his name.

To reach Wild Basin, take Colorado Route 7 south from Estes Park, about 5.0 miles past the road to the Longs Peak ranger station and campground. Copeland Lake marks the beginning of Wild Basin. It is here that the Sandbeach Lake trailhead is located. The trail begins on the northeast side of the lake and immediately starts up the side of Copeland Moraine. Don't get discouraged with the initial twenty minutes of this rocky trail, for it shortly levels off, and about one mile up the trail becomes quite pleasant. At 1.2 miles, the trail to Meeker Park (on Colorado Route 7) via the saddle between Lookout Mountain and Horsetooth Peak cuts off to the right. About 1.0 mile further up the trail is the Campers Creek campsite (GJ). An additional mile of hiking takes you to the Hunters Creek campsite (GE). The trail from here to Sandbeach Lake goes up for another mile. The campsites (GA) will be on your right as you drop down to the north side of the lake. This lake, like others in Wild Basin, was turned into a reservoir before the formation of the park. Before it was expanded into a reservoir in the early 1900s, it actually was a lake with a sandy beach. The name of this 10,000-foot body of water has tempted some to try swimming while camping here. The first and last person the author saw attempting this lasted somewhere between ten and fifteen seconds before making a remarkably swift retreat.

WILD BASIN TO THUNDER LAKE

Most of the Wild Basin area can be reached by starting at the Wild Basin ranger station, 3.0 miles past Copeland Lake on the dirt road running southwest. Although a relatively long hike–almost 7.0 miles–Thunder Lake is one of the more popular in the park. From the ranger station, the trail parallels

Near the shore of Thunder Lake. Boulder-Grand pass is at the very end of the valley. (Photograph by the author.)

the North Saint Vrain River almost all the way to beautiful Calypso Cascades, 1.8 miles from the trailhead. Here the trail forks. To the left, the Allens Park/Wild Basin trail connects with the Finch Lake/Pear Reservoir trail. The fork to the right, the Thunder Lake trail, crosses the bridges at the cascades. The Thunder Lake trail meanders up the densely wooded valley, past the Bluebird Lake trail junction on the left, for 1.3 miles to the North Saint Vrain campsite (GF), situated on a relatively flat area on the north side of the river. Another 1.3 miles and the Lion Lake trail cuts up to the right. Thunder Lake is 2.0 miles above this trail junction. The campsites (GB) are in the vicinity of the patrol cabin on the northeast side of the lake.

To reach the area just above Thunder Lake, go around the north side to the west. Shortly after leaving sight of Thunder, the trail ends. Falcon Lake and Lake of Many Winds are situated just below the continental divide. Between Pilot Mountain on your right and Tanima peak on the left is Boulder-

Grand Pass. The meadows between Thunder Lake and timberline, going west, are filled with alpine flowers and the scent of spruce trees pervades the air.

WILD BASIN TO GRAND LAKE

A popular, long trip is Wild Basin to Grand Lake, about 18.0 miles one way. From Thunder Lake, ascend to Lake of Many Winds and the base of Boulder-Grand Pass. Later in the season much of the snow on the eastern side of the steep pass has melted. You should climb up the right side of the draw, next to the ridge that descends from the top. Be extremely careful since the rock is loose and can be hazardous. From the pass the route goes cross-country without trail to the valley of the East Inlet. As the descent begins, Fifth Lake is to the south, with Fourth Lake, Spirit Lake, and Lake Verna, in that order, visible below. The trail into this area will be described in chapter 10, along with some variations on this same trip.

THE LAKES SOUTH OF THUNDER LAKE

A very isolated area of the park is on the south side of Tanima Peak from Thunder Lake. Four alpine lakes are found in this valley, south of Tanima and north of Mahana Peak. In order of appearance, they are Box Lake, Eagle Lake, and Frigid Lake, with tiny Indigo Pond nearby. Since there is no trail to them, bushwacking is necessary. Go south from Thunder Lake up the east flank of Tanima until the trees thin out. From this point, circumnavigate the ridge to the left, attempting to stay at about the same elevation. About 1.0 mile of walking brings you to Box Lake. The stream at the southwest side flows down from Eagle Lake, just above. The Eagles Beak is the rock formation directly west. Facing Eagles Beak, Frigid Lake is to the immediate left and Indigo Pond is on the right, up this small but impressive valley. Above Frigid Lake is Moomaw Glacier, a small body of ice named after a park ranger. Those bound for Frigid Lake should go up directly south from the west end of Eagle Lake to the flat tundra, and then to the right directly toward Moomaw Glacier. The rise in elevation between Box Lake and Frigid is 1,000 feet. The trip to Frigid Lake requires good conditioning and plenty of curiosity.

LION LAKE TRAIL

We now digress to the Lion Lake trail cutoff on the Thunder Lake trail. Lion Lake No. 1 (you guessed it, there are two of them) is 2.3 miles ahead on an occasionally indistinct and damp trail. Lion Lake No. 1 and the neighboring Lion Lake No. 2, Trio Falls, and Snowbank Lake occupy a rather flat expanse below Chiefs Head and Mount Alice. These peaks are occasionally climbed from this area.

From the area between Lion Lake No. 1 and Trio Falls, you can cut to the right (east) and head for Keplinger Lake. This remote lake is tucked away from the view of most Wild Basin visitors, at the base of Pagoda Mountain's south face. From Lion Lake No. 1, walk up the valley a short distance until the trees begin to disappear. At this point begin switchbacking up the North Ridge. As you approach the top, start heading north again across the open tundra. Your bearing should be directly toward the steep wall on Pagoda. Be sure to maintain your elevation. If you drop down to the valley on the east side of the North Ridge, you will only have to walk back up.

BLUEBIRD LAKE TRAIL

The Bluebird Lake trail cuts off from the Thunder Lake trail just over 3.0 miles from the trailhead. Ouzel Falls is on the Thunder Lake trail, about halfway between this trail cutoff and Calypso Cascades. Initially the trail goes up a few switchbacks, and then veers right, with Ouzel Creek on your left. About 1.0 mile of gentle trail takes you to a fork, the left proceeding 0.5 mile to Ouzel Lake, and the right 2.0 miles to Bluebird Lake. The campsite at Ouzel (GG) is on the north side of the lake, between the lake and Chickadee Pond. Bluebird Lake, about 6.5 miles from the trailhead, lies in a rugged valley flanked by Copeland Mountain on the south, Mahana Peak on the north, and Ouzel Peak on the west. The campsite here (GC) is a short distance below the lake, just past the Ouzel Creek crossing. Lark Pond and Pipit Lake lie directly west of Bluebird, the latter about 1.0 mile distant. Skirt Bluebird on the north side and start climbing up as you near the west end of the lake. On the left side of Ouzel Peak and due southwest from Bluebird is Junco Lake. Junco, too, is about 1.0 mile away, and is reached from the left side of Bluebird Lake. Go directly up the bottom of this steep, short valley to the flat tundra at Junco.

Bluebird is another of the Wild Basin lakes that was turned into a reservoir. Among the items packed in for construction of this lake in 1914 were bundles of reinforcing steel, a rock crusher, an automobile engine, and sacks upon sacks of cement. Backpackers who arrive at Bluebird Lake, having carried a mere thirty pounds might consider a reverent moment of silence for those poor mules and crazy dam builders—or damn crazy builders, if you prefer.

FINCH LAKE/PEAR RESERVOIR

The left fork off the Wild Basin trail is the route to Finch Lake and Pear Reservoir. Seven-tenths of a mile can be saved enroute to these lakes by beginning at Finch Lake trailhead, instead of Wild Basin ranger station. Finch Lake trailhead is shortly before the ranger station on the left side of the road from Copeland Lake. It is also accessible from points near the town of Allens Park and the park boundary. Finch Lake is either 4.5 or 5.2 miles in, depending on where you start. It is an easy, although somewhat uninteresting trail, and the lake and campsite (GL) is surrounded by trees, eliminating the view.

Pear Reservoir (a third Wild Basin reservoir), just over 2.0 miles above Finch Lake, indeed has more appealing views. The Pear Creek campsite (GH) is 0.3 mile from the reservoir, where campsite GD is located.

The valley above Pear Reservoir is the location of the Hutcheson Lakes, and, above them, Cony Lake. At least 2.0 miles of wild country, flanked by Elk Tooth on the south and Copeland Mountain on the north, must be traveled to reach remote Cony Lake at the base of Ogalalla Peak. The southern tip of Cony Lake is outside the park boundary, as are the summits of Elk Tooth and Ogalalla Peak.

MOUNTAINS OF WILD BASIN

Many of the peaks in Wild Basin are interesting climbs, although the approaches are some of the longest in the park. Mount Alice, for instance, via the Lion Lake trail, is nearly

20.0 miles round trip. Therefore, it is not feasible to attempt three or four mountains in a one-day trip, as in the vicinity of Flattop Mountain. Camping in Wild Basin the night before is practically a necessity to prevent utter fatigue.

PAGODA MOUNTAIN

Pagoda Mountain, 13,497 feet, which was mentioned in chapter 6, is approached via Sandbeach Lake. From the lake, start hiking cross-country north through the timber until you reach Hunters Creek. Follow this creek up along the north side. An unnamed lake at the base of a sharp ridge coming down from Pagoda is the junction of routes leading to Keplinger Lake (left) and Pagoda (right). Continue following the creek, which soon becomes a trickle, up the valley formed by Pagoda on your left and Longs-Meeker massif on the right. In early summer there is quite a bit of snow in the upper portions of this couloir, making the going easier than traveling on loose rock and talus later in the summer. A certain amount of route-finding skill is required to make the ascent to the Longs-Pagoda ridge and Keyboard of the Winds; caution is advised. At the ridge turn left and proceed up an additional 400 feet to the summit.

MOUNT MEEKER

Mount Meeker, 13,911 feet, described in chapter 6, can be approached from Wild Basin via the Sandbeach Lake trail. Leave the trail and go north at the Hunters Creek campsite (GE) or just before the slight descent is made to Sandbeach. In both cases, the route proceeds along the stream through the conspicuous south-sloping draw that forks into a *Y* near Dragons Egg Rock. Take the left fork up to the southwest ridge of Meeker, and then to the summit. This is a long trip, and it seems to get longer with every step up to the mountain. The summit is about four thousand feet higher than Hunters Creek campsite. It should be attempted only by those in very good shape.

CHIEFS HEAD PEAK

Chiefs Head Peak, 13,579 feet, is west of Pagoda, and divides Glacier Gorge and Wild Basin. It too can be approached from either area. The route from the north was discussed in chapter 6. The Wild Basin routes originate either in the vicinity of Sandbeach Lake or Lion Lake. From Sandbeach Lake, go along the north side of the shore and then directly west. The trees are shortly left behind, and Mount Orton is ascended amidst alpine meadows. Although it is not necessary to climb this peak, you may want to wander to its 11,724-foot summit. This summit is at the easterly end of the so-called North Ridge, which leads all the way to Chiefs Head. Keplinger Lake is visible halfway up this ridge on your right. An impressive wall of rock formed by the south ridge of Pagoda is directly behind it.

The other approach to Chiefs Head is also the best way of climbing Mount Alice, its neighbor to the southwest. Follow the Lion Lake trail to its end at Lion Lake No. 1, and then hike beyond it to Snowbank Lake. Then hike to the saddle at the end of this valley. From this point on the continental divide, it's a rather easy walk to the summit of Chiefs Head to the east. From the summit, Lake Powell is visible in the valley to the north.

MOUNT ALICE

Mount Alice, 13,310 feet, is climbed from this same saddle. From the summit of Chiefs Head, travel south to the beginning of the rocky northern ridge, and stay as high as the terrain permits. A few hundred feet below the summit of Mount Alice, the mountain seems to widen, and the steep west face disappears from view. For those who climb Mount Alice from Thunder Lake, the trip involves bushwacking through the forest to the open area north of the lake. Following the first significant stream you encounter, you eventually reach a fairly steep slope below the divide. This is just south of the route from Snowbank Lake, but does not present any problems. You can return to Thunder Lake either the same way, or, better yet, by going south from the summit of Mount Alice to Boulder-Grand Pass and then down. This route from Mount Alice via Boulder-Grand Pass also makes a good route up. It is probably the one to choose if Mount Alice is your only destination. Depending on the time of year, you will encounter

On the way to Falcon Lake. Pilot Mountain is on the left. In the background are high points along the continental divide, south of Mount Alice. (Photograph by the author.)

either steep snow or steep scree above Lake of Many Winds, so proceed up to the pass with care.*

TANIMA PEAK/PILOT MOUNTAIN

Tanima Peak, 12,420 feet, is only about four hundred feet above Boulder-Grand Pass, and can be easily climbed via that pass from Thunder Lake. Energetic hikers descending from Mount Alice will find the summit of Tanima only slightly out of their way.

Pilot Mountain, north of Tanima Peak, appears as a sharp rock outcropping. It is similar to the Little Matterhorn in that it is a ridge coming down from the divide, whose summit is one of the lower parts of the ridge. In fact, this "mountain" has no summit per se; it really isn't a mountain at all. Let's move on to one that is.

**Scree* is an accumulation of stones or rocky debris on a slope, or at the base of a hill.

ISOLATION PEAK

Isolation Peak, 13,118 feet, is one of the more isolated, more rewarding, peaks in Rocky Mountain National Park. The standard route involves making a base camp at the Bluebird Lake area. Traverse around Bluebird, and ascend to Pipit Lake. From Pipit go directly north, switchbacking up about six hundred feet and a bit less than 0.5 mile, to Isolation Lake, a small body of water on the saddle between Mahana Peak on the right and Isolation Peak on the left. Past this lake, the hiker will veer naturally to the left, up the steep draw to the top of the south ridge of Isolation. As you near this relatively flat spot on the ridge, an outcropping appears to the left. From here, it's a right turn north to the summit. From the pond on the saddle to the top is 1,000 feet, and it is climbed in a relatively short distance. Add to this the 1,400+ feet it takes to get from the Bluebird Lake campsite to the saddle, and it makes the summit cairn a rather relieving sight. Take your pack off, break out the instant lemonade, and take in one incredible view: Paradise Park to the west, the upper East Inlet on the north, the whole of Wild Basin on the east, and the Indian Peaks to the south. From the saddle between Mahana and Isolation Peaks, it's a relatively short hike, with little elevation loss down to the Eagles Beak and Frigid Lake. But, having climbed one of the park's more remote mountains, you may want to call it a day and head for camp.

OUZEL PEAK

Ouzel Peak, 12,716 feet, can be climbed by going past Bluebird as you would on the way to Isolation. At Lark Pond you can either go straight up the valley and climb to the divide between Isolation and Ouzel, or go south, switchbacking directly onto Ouzel's northeast ridge. On the latter route, it is recommended that you stay somewhat right of the crest of the ridgetop. A fair amount of experience is also advised. If you choose the Isolation-Ouzel ridge route, you will probably find it technically easier, although somewhat longer. South of Ouzel, just outside the park, along tundra reminicent of Flattop Mountain, is Ogalalla Peak, 13,138 feet.

Bluebird Lake. On the right is the east ridge of Ouzel Peak. Junco Lake sits on a rock shelf in the valley above the clouds. (Photograph courtesy of Peter Hammerschmidt.)

COPELAND MOUNTAIN

Copeland Mountain, 13,176 feet, is best approached from the campsite at Pear Reservoir. Walk around the lake on the east and north. At the far side of the reservoir, go directly north, essentially following the tree line. After passing a couple of small ponds on the right, the climb begins. Start up, continuing north until the terrain begins to level. This is the cue for a left turn, west. From this point be prepared for an awfully long 1.3 miles and a two-thousand-foot rise. From this mountain, as with many others, it is best to descend the way you came up. Since you have already found a passable route up, don't spend time looking for another one for the descent. The expansive eastern slope of Copeland is also accessible from Ouzel Lake by going directly south through the forest for about 0.8 mile.

Chapter 8

The Mummy Range

NORTH FORK AREA*

From Indianhead Ranch, elevation 7,840 feet, to:

DESTINATION	MILEAGE	ELEVATION (ft.)
Halfway campsite	6.3	9,360
Husted trail junction	6.5	8,530
Lake Husted	11.0	11,088
Lake Louise	11.5	11,030
Lost Falls	8.0	9,800
Lost Lake	10.3	10,714
Lost Meadows campsite	9.0	10,380
North Fork ranger station	6.0	9,280
North Fork trail	6.0	9,280
Northern Park boundary	12.5	10,400
Park boundary (from McGraw)	3.8	10,400
Stormy Peaks Pass	10.3	11,600
Stormy Peaks trail junction	8.3	9,960
West Creek trail	1.5	7,880

LONG DRAW RESERVOIR AREA

From Big South trailhead at Corral Creek, elevation 10,000 feet, to:

DESTINATION	MILEAGE	ELEVATION (ft.)
Koenig campsites	5.0	10,700
Mirror Lake	5.8	11,000
Mirror Lake trail junction	4.3	10,700
Mummy Pass	6.0	11,250
Mummy Pass Creek campsites	4.3	10,680
North boundary	8.3	10,400

*When starting at Dunraven trailhead, subtract 3.0 miles for destinations above North Fork ranger station.

Part of the Mummy Range. This is a view from the side of Twin Sisters. From left to right are Mount Chicquita, Ypsilon Mountain, and Fairchild Mountain. (Photograph by the author.)

MUMMY RANGE AREA

From Lawn Lake trailhead, elevation 8,500 feet, to:

DESTINATION	MILEAGE	ELEVATION (ft.)
Chipmunk Lake	4.0	10,640
Crystal Lake	7.8	11,480
Jay Lakes (highest one)	5.8	11,200
Lawn Lake/Ypsilon trail junction	1.3	9,200
Roaring River campsites	1.5	9,200
Spectacle Lakes (lowest one)	5.0	11,350
Tileston Meadows campsite	6.0	10,780
The Saddle	8.0	12,398
Ypsilon Creek campsite	2.3	9,540
Ypsilon Lake	4.5	10,520

TRAILS IN THE MUMMY RANGE

The Arapaho referred to the mountains of the Mummy Range as the "White Owls." This name seems particularly appropriate when viewing them on quiet moonlit nights. The Mummy Range derives its name from an imaginative early Estes Park visitor who thought it resembled an Egyptian mummy. The upper part is presumably Mummy Mountain. If, on viewing this range, that seems absurd, then wait until dark and try visualizing a bear in the Big Dipper. "That which we call a rose by any other name would smell as sweet."*

LAWN LAKE TRAIL

The geographical area of this chapter lies north of Trail Ridge Road, from Estes Park on the east to Fall River on the west. Its numerous campsites attest to its popularity for hiking and backpacking. The Lawn Lake trail is the most well used leading into the Mummys. The Lawn Lake trailhead in Horseshoe Park is most directly reached by going west on U.S. Route 34, through the Fall River entrance. Just west of Sheep Lakes, take a right at the signs indicating Endovalley picnic area. The Lawn Lake trailhead is on your immediate right.

The trail, initially rather steep, switchbacks a short distance up the lower reaches of Bighorn Mountain, 11,463 feet, directly to the north. Within 0.5 mile, the trail begins to level slightly as you begin walking into denser timber. At 1.5 miles from the trailhead, you reach the Lawn Lake-Ypsilon Lake trailhead, with the Roaring River campsite (CD) close by. From this point to Lawn Lake (CA), the trail parallels the Roaring River. About a mile of gradual trail brings you to campsites CC and CF, the former at the junction of Roaring River and Ypsilon Creek. Both campsites are located on Ypsilon Creek, not on the Ypsilon Lake trail. Three sets of switchbacks and 2.0-2.5 miles later is the Big Rock campsite (CE). Just above is the first of two open areas on the trail below Lawn Lake. At the second open area, a cutoff to the right leads to Potts Puddle and Black Canyon. Lawn Lake is a short distance past this point, 6.2 miles from the trailhead.

The 1961 USGS map shows two squares, or structures, at Lawn Lake. A patrol cabin is still near the lake, but the other structure, a shelter cabin, was removed in 1964. On the east side of Lawn Lake is a dam, built in 1911.

From Lawn Lake, looking northwest, is The Saddle, with Hagues Peak on the right and Fairchild Mountain on the left. The rock wall sloping up on the right side of Fairchild is part of a spectacular cirque, where Crystal and Little Crystal lakes

*William Shakespeare, *Romeo and Juliet,* act 2, sc. 2, lines 44-45.

lie. This is an interesting hike, and is only 1.5 miles from Lawn Lake. To get to these lakes, continue on the trail on the north side of Lawn Lake. A short distance past Lawn Lake, as you begin to gain elevation, is the left turn to Little Crystal and Crystal lakes. The trail to Crystal Lake is reminiscent of that to Sky Pond, with the rock slabs, boulders, and cairns. The round trip to Lawn Lake is about 12.5 miles and to Crystal, about 15.5.

Potts Puddle is about 1.0 mile southeast of the Lawn Lake trail, and sits on the saddle between Mount Tileston on the south and Mummy Mountain on the north. This small lake is near the Tileston Meadows campsite (CB) and about 0.5 mile above the Lower Tileston Meadows campsite (CG), both near Black Canyon Creek.

BLACK CANYON TRAIL

Potts Puddle and Lawn Lake are accessible via the Black Canyon trail, originating at the McGraw Ranch. McGraw Ranch, or as it is now called, Indianhead Ranch, is north of Estes Park, and is reached via a road off of the Devil's Gulch Road. This route to Potts Puddle and vicinity is nearly 2.0 miles longer than the Lawn Lake trail, and frankly offers little in terms of view or interesting terrain. However, it may be desirable as an out-of-the-way route.

YPSILON LAKE TRAIL

The Ypsilon Lake trail cuts off from the Lawn Lake trail about 1.3 miles from the trailhead. After a gradual run south, it cuts to the right and begins to rise in elevation along a ridge. This continues for about 1.5 miles, and then again becomes more gradual. At the 4.0-mile mark, tiny Chipmunk Lake appears off to the right amid thick timber. Ypsilon Lake, considerably smaller than Lawn, is 0.5 mile away. Just before you reach the lake, you must descend about one hundred fifty feet.

Above and to the west is Mount Chiquita. The remarkable rock face to its right, and northwest of the lake, is Ypsilon Mountain, so named for the *Y*-shaped couloir on the east face. (Ypsilon is the Greek letter for *Y*.) Fairchild Mountain is directly north, and Mummy Mountain appears to the northeast.

Just above Ypsilon Lake, you can leave the trail and continue toward the face of Ypsilon Mountain. This will shortly lead you to the creek draining from Chiquita and Spectacle lakes above. Follow the creek directly west about 0.8 mile to Chiquita Lake. To reach Spectacle Lakes, follow the creek that flows into the one from Chiquita from the north. The first of the Spectacle Lakes is about 0.5 mile away through some rough country in the great cirque of Ypsilon Mountain. On the other side of the northern wall of this cirque are the Fay Lakes, the habitat of the greenbacked cutthroat trout. Since this is an endangered species, fishing is totally prohibited.

The body of a climber killed in an accident in 1902 is buried 700 feet above Spectacle Lakes in a coffin of iron plates. During the writing of this book, another fatality occured in the Ypsilon *Y* couloir. These are sobering reminders of the risks involved in climbing such rock faces.

NORTH FORK/NORTH BOUNDARY TRAILS

North of the Black Canyon trail is a system of trails, of which the North Fork or Dunraven trail is the most important. This trail leads to the high lakes of the North Fork of the Big Thompson River. It begins at a forest service trailhead reached by a dirt road about 1.5 miles below Glen Haven. This road is on the north side of the road from Glen Haven to Drake, and extends through Dunraven Glade for about 3.0 miles to the trailhead. From there, you walk through thick timber for about 2.5 miles to the national park boundary, and an additional mile to the North Fork ranger station, where the Dunraven and North Boundary trails meet. The Dunraven trail is the shortest route into the valley of the North Fork of the Big Thompson.

However, some hikers may elect to make a longer trip by taking the North Boundary trail. If you desire to begin hiking at Indianhead Ranch (formerly McGraw Ranch), you should contact the ranch for permission to park your vehicle, as it is private property and not a park trailhead. From Indianhead Ranch, it is a long way (10.5 miles) to Lost Lake. The trail leaves the ranch, climbs abruptly, and then descends just as quickly to the crossing at West Creek. Two and one-half miles from the start is the dead-end Husted trail, near the Fox Creek crossing. Up to this point, you will have been walking in Roosevelt National Forest, but very shortly you enter the park. Over 3.0 miles of up and down hiking takes you to the North Fork ranger station. Here the trail meets the Dunraven trail. Take the left fork toward Lost Lake. Four and one-third miles west along the North Fork of the Big Thompson is Lost Lake, with the south face of Sugarloaf Mountain on your right. The Lost Lake campsite (BA) is on the south side of the river, just before the lake. Consult the map in the map section for the locations of the other campsites along the North Fork on this route to Lost Lake.

SIGNAL MOUNTAIN TRAIL

This region is also accessible from the Signal Mountain trail, beginning at Pingree Park, the location of Colorado State University's summer forestry campus. Pingree Park is north of the park, and is reached by traveling up the Poudre Canyon west of Fort Collins. The Pingree Park road (improved gravel) goes south from Poudre Canyon and is well marked. The Signal Mountain trail originates along the Pingree Park road, and follows Pennock Creek to the Signal Mountain/South Signal Mountain area on the extreme northeast corner of the park. The Stormy Peaks trail from Pingree Park ascends near the South Fork of the Poudre River (known more formally as the Cache la Poudre) for about 5.0 miles until Stormy Peaks (12,135 feet) and Stormy Peaks Pass. West is a long, flat area, the high point of which is the summit of Sugarloaf Mountain. Across the valley to the south is a ridge with three high points. As viewed from the pass, Mount Dunraven, 12,571 feet, is to the right, while Mount Dickinson, 11,831 feet, is on the left. The one in the middle is unnamed, although its elevation is greater than Dickinson by almost 500 feet.

One and a half miles down from Stormy Peaks Pass is the juncture of Stormy Peaks trail and South Signal Mountain trail. Just before the trail junction is the Stormy Peaks South campsite (BD). A short but quick descent, and we are in the valley of the North Fork. Two miles west is Lost Lake. One-half mile above Lost Lake is Lake Husted, and another 0.5 mile, Lake Louise. Lake Dunraven is just south of Lake Louise, another 0.5 mile or so along the North Fork. Above

Lake Louise to the west is Icefield Pass, at the saddle between Skull Point and Rowe Mountain, to the north and south, respectively.

MUMMY PASS TRAIL

The Mummy Pass trail also originates in the Pingree Park area, and leads to Mummy Pass, about 2.0 miles west of Icefield Pass. North of Mummy Pass is Fall Mountain, 12,258 feet, located on a ridge leading to Commanche Peak outside the park. The trail west from Mummy Pass leads down into the trees, with Hague Creek below on the left. At Mummy Pass Creek is the Mummy Pass Creek campsite (HC), and shortly thereafter, the cutoff to the right to the Koenig campsite (HD). Mirror Lake is about 1.0 mile beyond at the beginning of the prominent cirque, just to the north. At the confluence of the Poudre River and Hague Creek, and roughly 3.0 miles west of the Mummy Pass Creek campsite, is the Hague Creek campsite (HA). This north-central area of this park is most easily reached from the road leading up to Long Draw Reservoir, just outside the park. However, this requires a very long drive almost all the way up Poudre Canyon.

CHAPIN CREEK TRAIL

Camping areas are also found along the Chapin Creek trail. Drive west from the Lawn Lake trailhead and up Fall River Road. Chapin Pass is a short distance north of a marked trailhead on the right, more than three-fourths of the way up Fall River Road, just above Willow Park and a series of switchbacks in the road. The trail is steep for about five minutes until Chapin Pass is reached. It then drops off to the north into a tree-lined valley. Since bogs are common at the first part of the trail, your hiking boots should be waterproofed. The Chapin group site (HE) and the Cache campsite (HB) are about 3.5 and 4.0 miles north, respectively. This trail eventually passes the campsite at Hague Creek (HA), and continues on as the Big South trail to Poudre Canyon.

To the east, up toward the mountains from Chapin Creek, lies the Chapin Creek cross-country zone (3H), a convenient place to camp for climbing Chapin, Chiquita, Ypsilon, and Desolation. Another cross-country zone (2H) extends from the Hague Creek drainage to the north side of Flatiron Mountain and Desolation Peaks.

MOUNTAINS OF THE MUMMY RANGE

The most popular mountains of the Mummy Range are those that can be seen from the vicinity of Estes Park and Trail Ridge Road. Due to the remoteness and the less spectacular nature of the unseen mountains bordering the valley of the North Fork, fewer hikers venture there.

HAGUES/MUMMY/FAIRCHILD

Three more prominent peaks, Hagues Peak, Mummy Mountain, and Fairchild Mountain, are perhaps the most climbed mountains in the Mummy Range. They are readily accessible from Lawn Lake. Hagues Peak, 13,560 feet, the fourth highest in the park, is reached via the trail from Lawn Lake to The Saddle. As you near the bottom of the southwest ridge of Hagues, and the trail ends, go up the ridge to the right. The western flank of this ridge is quite impressive.

Mummy Mountain, 13,425 feet, is often climbed in conjunction with Hagues. From the top of Hagues Peak, walk along the gradual east ridge for just over 1.0 mile, descending about 600 feet to the saddle between the two mountains. One-half mile more to the southeast, and a climb of 500 feet, brings you to the summit of Mummy Mountain.

For those who wish only to climb Mummy, there are two routes. The first is to proceed around Lawn Lake and head toward The Saddle between Fairchild and Hagues, as previously described. When you reach a point almost due north of Little Crystal Lake and near the stream crossing, turn right and northeast toward the Hagues/Mummy saddle, and hike up from there. The alternative route is to go east from Lawn Lake, taking the trail toward Potts Puddle. After the initial set of switchbacks, go north (left) through the sparse timber and the lower reaches of Mummy's south ridge. One and a half miles and 2,200 feet away is the summit. This route is less interesting than the first, but may be appealing to those making their second ascent and seeking a different route.

Fairchild Mountain, 13,502 feet, is the third peak forming

Mummy Mountain. Lawn Lake sits just below the snowfield on Mummy Mountain's south face. (Photograph courtesy of Tom Nilsson.)

the Lawn Lake/Crystal Lake valley. The route to Fairchild is again up the trail from Lawn Lake to The Saddle at the western end of the valley. The summit is left along the tundra about 1.0 mile. For the best views, stay to the right along the ridge.

THE ROWES

Rowe Peak, 13,400 feet, Rowe Mountain, 13,184 feet, and Rowe Glacier are in a relatively tight cluster directly north of the summit of Hagues Peak. For this reason, the most practical way of visiting the area is to go over the summit of Hagues. Since the hike to the Rowes is an advanced one, it should be undertaken only by those in good shape.

As viewed from Hagues, Rowe Peak is an inconspicuous high point on the north side of the glacier below, at the end of the extremely jagged ridge on the left. This type of ridge separating two gorges is called an arête. Rowe Glacier has diminished remarkably in size since its discovery by a bear hunter, Israel Rowe, in 1880. Early photos reveal that at that time the ice almost totally filled the small cirque it occupies today. Rowe Peak is climbed from Hagues by descending and going around to the east side of the glacial lake. From here, walking up the northern side of the glacier to the flat summit, is an elevation gain of about 500 feet. Rowe Mountain is 0.5 mile north and is, in fact, only a ridge of Rowe Peak.

Incidentally, the creek flowing out of the tarn at Rowe Glacier is the beginning of the North Fork of the Big Thompson. For those who are looking for a multiple-day trip in the Mummys, the descent to lakes Louise, Husted, and Lost, makes for a good second day, after a day at Lawn. If you make this trip, you may want to avoid Hagues Peak's summit, and pass instead over the Mummy/Hagues saddle. Once on top, keep heading due north and drop down into the valley beginning at Rowe Peak. Follow the stream down past a series of ponds to Lake Dunraven. This is a beautiful alpine lake with a view to match, but unfortunately camping is not allowed here. Camping is permitted at Lost Lake, however, and it is only about 1.5 miles away. Lake Dunraven is also a pleasant side trip for those camped at Lost Lake, who have approached from the Dunraven trail below.

MOUNT DUNRAVEN/MOUNT DICKINSON

Mount Dunraven, 12,571 feet, and Mount Dickinson, 11,831 feet, if not approached from the Lost Lake area to the north, can be climbed via the Hagues/Mummy saddle. Just

The Mummy Range from Horseshoe Park. From left to right are Mount Chapin, Mount Chiquita, Ypsilon Mountain, and Fairchild Mountain. The Lawn Lake trailhead is at the right. (Photograph courtesy of the National Park Service.)

remember that the round trip from the Lawn Lake trailhead to Dunraven is 8.0 miles, and about 12.0 for Dickinson. Also keep in mind that from the Lawn Lake trailhead to the summits of these mountains, there is a vertical rise of some 5,000 feet. This is as much as the vertical rise from the Longs Peak ranger station to the top of Longs Peak. Therefore, don't be deceived by the somewhat less rugged appearance of the mountains of the Mummys. It's still a lot of work in terms of elevation gain and distance covered.

CHAPIN/CHIQUITA/YPSILON

Mount Chapin, 12,454 feet, Mount Chiquita, 13,069 feet, and Ypsilon Mountain, 13,514 feet, are situated south of Fairchild Mountain and north of the Fall River Road. Before this road was reopened to vehicle travel, these peaks were usually climbed via Fall River Pass and the Alpine Visitor Center, making them considerably more isolated. Now, these three, which can be climbed in one-day trips, are reached by first driving to the Chapin Creek trailhead on the Fall River Road. As described previously, the trail to the Chapin Creek campsites goes up a steep, but short, section to Chapin Pass, the highest point on this trail. At this point, turn right and follow a very faint trail east. Shortly, you begin to break into the sparse growth around the timberline. To climb Chapin, continue up and directly east through intermittent clumps of dense, dwarfed alpine spruce. These patches of spruce are reduced in size to bushes growing in wind-sheltered areas, known as Krummholz growth or wind timber. Above you is what appears to be the top, but this is a false summit 60 feet below and 0.5 mile west of the true summit. From this false summit, there is a good view of the forbidding south face of Chapin. Deep gashes and rock spires abound, as well as a good view of the true summit. To ascend the true summit of Chapin, simply skirt the edge of the south face along the gentle slope.

Descending from Chapin about 400 feet north takes you to a saddle. Continuing 0.8 mile north, and nearly 1,000 feet up, you will reach the summit of Mount Chiquita. One mile north is Ypsilon Mountain. Descend 200 feet to the Chiquita/Ypsilon saddle, and follow the ridge up again, roughly 700 feet in elevation. The view from the top of Ypsilon toward Spectacle Lakes over the *Y* couloir is reminiscent of Chasm Lake from parts of Longs Peak.

DESOLATION PEAKS/FLATIRON MOUNTAIN

Desolation Peaks, 12,949 feet, and Flatiron Mountain, 12,335 feet, are occasionally overlooked by climbers in favor of the more conspicuous Chapin-Chiquita-Ypsilon chain. The route to Desolation initially duplicates that of Chapin. As you begin to leave the trees above Chapin Pass, start veering to your left, and begin moving north along the west side of Mount Chapin. It is best to stay as level in your traverse as possible, and near timberline. After you pass the third creek, about 2.5 miles from the start, take switchbacks up a long steep draw east. You will recognize this draw because, in addition to being the third drainage system, it is situated just prior to where the route takes a noticeable swing to the left. At the tip of the ridge, Desolation is clearly visible across the gorge below you. Follow this ridge up about 0.5 mile. Just before the Desolation ridge meets the one you have been walking on, there is a rise in elevation. You can either go up and then right, to the crest of the Desolation ridge, or cut right immediately, working toward the summit spire along the south face of the ridge. In either case be extremely careful. This rock breaks easily, so watch for loose rock and poor hand- and footholds. At the end of the ridge, just below the summit, you must climb up a crack between two rocks (called a chimney) to reach the summit register. Although this can be a hazardous climb, Desolation Peak is an exciting trip.

Flatiron Mountain is northwest of Desolation about 1.5 miles, and can be very easily reached from the western end of the Desolation summit ridge. Hazeline Lake, on the north side of Flatiron, is one of the more remote lakes in the park. If you climb Flatiron, you may want to consider a return through the forest along the creek on the west side of the Chapin Creek trail, and then south to Chapin Pass. Both of these mountains offer a full day of hiking. The round trip to Desolation alone is 9.0-10.0 miles.

All the mountains, from Chapin north to Flatiron, have an advantage over those accessible from the Lawn Lake trailhead. At Chapin Creek trailhead, the usual starting point, you are almost 2,500 feet higher, and very close to timberline. Also, with the reopening of Fall River Road, the distance to these peaks has been cut down considerably. Overnight camping can be arranged in the Chapin Creek cross-country zone (3H), north of Chapin Pass, making them somewhat easier climbs.

Chapter 9

Along the Divide: Milner Pass to Bighorn Flats

NORTH AND SOUTH FROM MILNER PASS

From Milner Pass/Poudre Lake, elevation 10,750 feet, to:

DESTINATION	MILEAGE	ELEVATION (ft.)
Arrowhead Lake	4.5	11,320
Chapin Creek campsite	5.5	10,240
Forest Canyon Pass via Ute Trail	2.3	11,300
Hague Creek campsites	9.0	9,760
Mount Ida	4.5	12,880
Specimen Mountain	2.3	12,429
From Timber Lake trailhead on Trail Ridge Road, elevation 9,000 feet, to:		
Jackstraw campsite	4.0	10,750
Julian Lake	6.8	11,080
Rockslide campsite	4.5	10,960
Snowbird campsite	4.5	11,000
Timber Creek campsite	3.5	10,300
Timber Lake	5.3	11,040
From Green Mountain trailhead on Trail Ridge Road, elevation 8,800 feet, to:		
Bear Lake	16.0	9,475
Big Meadows	2.0	9,400
Granite Falls	5.5	9,800
Onahu/Timber Creek trail junction	4.0	9,650
Timber Creek campsite	5.8	10,300
Timberline campsite	6.5	10,560
Tonahutu Meadows campsite	5.5	10,050

Hayden Spire in Hayden Gorge. Below is the deep valley of Forest Canyon. The photo is taken from a point near Trail Ridge Road. (Photograph courtesy of Tom Post.)

LAKES IN THE AREA

The Milner Pass to Big Horn Flats area lies south of Trail Ridge Road, and includes the huge Forest Canyon, Gorge Lakes, Hayden Gorge, as well as the mountains along the continental divide. Some mention will also be made in this chapter of features along Trail Ridge Road, including the Ute Trail. This area of the park, although one of the most accessible, is one of the least traveled. There are two main reasons for this. First, the distance required to reach parts of the region is quite long. Second, this country is quite rugged, and lacks trails in certain areas, such as Forest Canyon. Overnight camping in this area is primarily along Timber Creek trail and in Forest Canyon, the largest cross-country camping zone in the park (1D).

THE GORGE LAKES

One of the most popular areas along this part of the divide is around the Gorge Lakes. Some of these lakes, which are flanked by steep mountains, are visible from Trail Ridge Road, most notably Rock Cut and Forest Canyon Overlook. There are two commonly accepted methods of reaching the Gorge Lakes. The first is to descend Forest Canyon directly from Trail Ridge Road. Many switchbacks are required to reach the Big Thompson River at the bottom of the canyon, and once tree line is encountered, much of that is over fallen timber. From the river, the creek coming out of the Gorge Lakes can be followed up to an open meadow. The stream forks, and the left branch leads east to Forest Lake, maybe 0.3 mile away. Continuing up the creek to the right takes you past Little Rock and Rock lakes. After these two smaller bodies of water, you reach the main Gorge Lakes at the beginning of a shelf higher up the valley, about 0.5 mile away. Arrowhead Lake, visible from Trail Ridge Road, is encountered first. Love Lake is just north of Arrowhead, and Doughnut Lake is to the south. Further up the shelf are Inkwell and Azure lakes, with usually frozen Highest Lake almost all the way up on the divide. Fishing is reputed to be excellent in these lakes, and the scenery is hard to beat. But the return up the side of Forest Canyon is grueling.

A better route to and from the Gorge Lakes begins at the Gore Range Overlook on Trail Ridge Road, between Iceberg Lake and the Alpine Visitor Center at Fall River Pass. Descend from the parking area to a couple of small ponds at Forest Canyon Pass. This route follows part of the old Ute Trail. At the pass, turn left and begin walking over tundra along the south side of Forest Canyon. If you stay at a reasonably constant elevation, the trip will be less exerting, though somewhat longer. After the first creek or obvious drainage, the route flattens out to an area of several small alpine ponds. The side of Mount Ida is visible straight ahead. When you encounter the steepness of this ridge, veer to the left and up. As you reach the crest of the ridge, Arrowhead Lake and the other Gorge Lakes stretch below you. The route round trip from the Gore Range Overlook is over 6.5 miles, compared to about 3.0 via the Forest Canyon descent route. Though somewhat longer, the Gore Range Overlook route is considerably less strenuous.

HAYDEN GORGE

Hayden Gorge is the valley southeast of the Gorge Lakes over the Cracktop/Mount Julian/Terra Tomah ridge. It lies almost wholly within the Forest Canyon cross-country zone (1D). For reasons mentioned at the beginning of this chapter, it is an extremely remote valley. If you're after seclusion, this is the place to camp. Hayden Spire is the sharp rock precipice at the end of this valley. The valley is formed by the Cracktop to Terra Tomah group on your right, and massive Stones Peak on your left. As you view Hayden Spire from the gorge, Lonesome Lake is on its left and Hayden Lake on the right. Routes to both lakes present no real problems. You can reach Hayden Lake from Forest Canyon, either from the Gorge Lakes area or from Trail Ridge Road. A more precarious, though feasible, route is down the south side of Cracktop, along the stream that flows into the unnamed pond near Hayden Lake. This entails camping in Hayden Gorge as a part of a multiday trip, some of which takes you along the continental divide.

TIMBER LAKE TRAIL

A much more accessible area, flanking the continental divide, is along the Timber Lake trail, originating on Trail Ridge Road in northern Kawuneeche Valley. This six-mile stretch of Trail Ridge Road, from Milner Pass toward Grand Lake, offers a unique panoramic view of the Never Summer Mountains. Jackstraw Mountain, just south of Milner Pass, can be seen on the east side of the highway. It was named Jackstraw for the large number of dead logs strewn on its western slope, evidence of an 1872 forest fire that consumed almost the whole side of the mountain.

From the Timber Lake trailhead the following campsites are accessible: Timber Creek (KA), at 3.5 miles; Jackstraw (KB), at 4.0 miles; Rockslide (KC), at 4.5 miles; and Snowbird (KD), at 4.6 miles. This last campsite is just below Timber Lake, which sits in a little valley on the west side of

Mount Ida. The trail is easy, with no difficult stretches, except for a set of switchbacks between the first and second campsites. Although the view along the trail isn't spectacular, Timber Lake is a pleasant spot, and this trail shouldn't be passed off as lightweight.

There is a discrepancy between the actual trail, and the way it appears on the map. Shortly past the Timber Creek campsite (KA) is a right fork to Long Meadows. The map shows this trail junction as further up than it actually is. The switchbacks begin at this junction, and continue for ten to fifteen minutes hiking time. The trail to Long Meadows from the Timber Lake trail is about 0.8 mile and somewhat poor. At Long Meadow, the trail continues as the Timber Creek trail for 1.5 miles along the east side of the meadow. This so-called trail is very indistinct, so simply stay on the left side of the meadow as you're headed south.

ONAHU CREEK

At the far end of Long Meadows is the beginning of a descent down to Onahu Creek and three campsites along the Onahu Creek trail.* At the junction of the trails going along Onahu Creek and Big Meadows (south) is the Onahu Bridge campsite (KG). Down Onahu Creek about 1.0 mile are the Upper Onahu and Onahu Creek sites (KF, KE). These campsites are more easily approached from the Onahu Creek trailhead on Trail Ridge Road, roughly 6.0 miles south of the Timber Lake trailhead.

Here is another area where the maps are misleading. The eighty-foot contour interval map of the park for this chapter shows a fork in the trail due east of Chickaree Lake. The northern fork supposedly goes up the south end of Long Meadows. This trail no longer exists. Instead, the trail continues up Onahu Creek to the Onahu Bridge campsite (KG). Also, the trail between Long Meadows and Onahu Bridge is further east and has more switchbacks than shown.

**Onahu,* incidentally, is the Arapaho Indian word for "warms himself." According to legend, *Onahu* was the name of an Arapaho horse that warmed itself by campfires on cold nights.

LONG MEADOWS CROSS-COUNTRY ZONE

You can camp on the east side of Long Meadows in the cross-country zone (1K), as indicated on the map at the beginning of this chapter. This is convenient for overnight stays below Julian Lake. The best way to get to Julian is via the Timber Lake trail. Once you reach Timber Lake, work your way around the south side, toward the saddle that rises at the end of the valley. After a steep climb to this saddle, Julian can be seen below. Though the descent to Julian necessitates slow travel over a boulder-strewn basin, it is well worth the effort. Cross-country camping in these upper reaches on Onahu Creek is great. Across this valley is another saddle, over which are the Haynach Lakes. Since this area is in the upper Tonahutu Creek drainage, it will be discussed in chapter 10.

MOUNTAINS OF THE REGION

MOUNT IDA

With one exception, most of the mountains of this area are climbed infrequently. The one exception is Mount Ida, 12,880+ feet, and two routes exist for its ascent. One begins at Milner Pass. From the parking lot, start walking east, up into the trees. Because of the steepness, switchbacking will help. Shortly after you begin, you will cross the Ute Trail. Continue up through the trees to timberline, about 0.5 mile from the parking lot. Skirt around the summit of the first rise on the tundra, and then crank out the miles along the extended ridge of the continental divide to the summit of Mount Ida. This is a good 4.0-4.5 miles, with no trail, along an open ridge. However, the lack of trail above timberline on tundra doesn't make for difficult walking.

The other route to Mount Ida, by way of the Timber Lake trail, is the best route if combined with an overnight stay. Camping the night before at the Jackstraw campsite (KB) is ideal. To reach Ida, begin at the upper end of the large open area at the Jackstraw campsite. Follow the first creek you come to on the trail at the end of this meadow. It will lead to another meadow, above on the east side of Jackstraw

Mountain, 11,704 feet. When you reach this meadow, start veering to the right and then go up. It's a little steep, and probably wet at first, but it becomes more gradual above timberline. Keep going east and a bit south to the summit of Ida. You can return the way you came or by an alternate route. If you choose the alternate way, hike down toward the saddle between Timber Lake and Julian Lake. The descent is gradual at first, but later becomes more steep. When you get close to Timber Lake, work your way around to the Timber Lake trail via the south side of the lake. Follow the trail back to the trailhead on Trail Ridge Road. This alternative is also a feasible route for the ascent of Ida.

Mount Ida is one of the best places in the park to see the elusive alpine grouse, the ptarmigan. Its camouflage is so excellent that it is possible to stare at a whole covey of them from ten feet away and see only one or two, assuming they remain still. Conies, small alpine rodents with rounded ears, are also in evidence on Mount Ida. Even if you don't see them, you will certainly hear them. Their high-pitched squeaks can be mistaken for the chirps of birds.

The summit of Mount Ida offers one of the finest views in Rocky Mountain National Park. The entire Never Summer Range is to the west. South, you can easily see Shadow Mountain Lake and the tip of Grand Lake, with Big Meadows and Long Meadows intervening. Julian Lake is just below on one side, and the upper Gorge Lakes are on the other. The Mummy Range is visible past Trail Ridge Road to the north, and southeast are dozens of mountains in the Bear Lake/Glacier Gorge/Wild Basin area. Any discomfort experienced while making the climb is quickly forgotten amidst the unbelievable grandeur.

CRACKTOP/MOUNT JULIAN/TERRA TOMAH

On the east side of the Gorge Lakes and extending out from the divide are Cracktop, 12,760+ feet, Mount Julian, 12,928 feet, and, Terra Tomah Mountain, 12,718 feet. From Mount Ida, descend the east side down the ridge. It is steep and rocky, but presents no technical problems. From the initial low point on the ridge, about 500 feet down, work your way back up and along the ridge at the head of the

From Trail Ridge Road looking south toward the valley of the Gorge Lakes. On the left is Mount Julian, and center-right is Cracktop. Highest Lake is below the large snowfield at the top right. (Photograph by the author.)

gorge. Highest Lake is just below the ridge on your left. Cracktop is the first high point on the ridge extension after this lake. Although the stretch from Ida to Cracktop is relatively short, it requires some time, as it resembles the difficulty of The Little Matterhorn ridge. Similarly, the route from Cracktop to the next mountain, Julian, is rough and exposed as well. But, a modicum of mountaineering skill and route-finding will suffice. From Mount Julian, the route to Terra Tomah seems like walking on a highway, compared to the country you have traversed to this point. The Cracktop to Terra Tomah group, though not difficult in a technical sense, is exhausting because of the up and down climbing. If you plan on reaching Terra Tomah via a campsite near Timber Lake, you should plan to leave at sunrise.

SPRAGUE MOUNTAIN/STONES PEAK

Stones Peak, 12,922 feet, is a massive mountain north of Bighorn Flats, from which it is approached. The route to Stones Peak and its neighbor on the divide, Sprague Moun-

Mount Terra Tomah from Forest Canyon overlook on Trail Ridge Road. (Photograph courtesy of Tom Post.)

tain, 12,713 feet, begins at Bear Lake. Make the previously described climb to Flattop Mountain. Take the right fork at the top, and proceed north as you would to Knobtop and Gabletop mountains. But this time continue across Bighorn Flats toward Sprague Mountain. You will probably pass an old water diversion project, Eureka Ditch, on the way to Sprague Pass at the head of Spruce Canyon on the right. Continue along the divide up the ridge to the summit of Sprague Mountain. Along the way you pass the top of Sprague Glacier, and can see three lakes directly below. The one near the glacier is a tarn.* Irene Lake and Rainbow Lake (the larger of the two) are below the tarn. Hourglass Lake is further east, against the side of Stones Peak.

From Sprague Mountain, start walking out onto the ridge, slightly left of the crest, to Stones. You will initially drop 500 feet, and then climb about 750 feet before reaching the final ridge to the summit. Coming back up that 500-foot

*A *tarn* is a steep-banked mountain lake formed by glacial action.

stretch on the return trip will not be one of your fond remembrances about this climb.

A shorter route to Stones, though a difficult one, is via the trail from the Fern Lake trailhead to Spruce Lake, as described. From Spruce Lake continue through the thick timber into Spruce Canyon, and veer left, following the south side of the valley up toward timberline. At this point turn north and climb up to the basin below the Sprague/Stones ridge halfway between Hourglass and Rainbow lakes. This, like all routes to Stones Peak, is steep, and requires good conditioning. Overnight camping is permitted in Spruce Canyon, since it is in the Forest Canyon cross-country zone (1D). Since the round trip to Stones Peak is, depending on the route, 17.0 to 21.0 miles, overnight camping is suggested.

Camping in the upper Tonahutu Creek area (see chapter 10) is also feasible as a base camp for the Sprague/Stones trip, although the upper campsite is 7.5 to 10.5 miles above any trailhead.

THE UTE TRAIL

The Ute trail runs from the western side of Beaver Meadows, at the eastern entrance to the park, to Kawuneeche Valley, north of Grand Lake. It parallels Trail Ridge Road for much of the way, occasionally crossing it. It presents a long but unique one-way hike. Just how much of this trail was followed by its alleged originators, the Ute and Arapaho, is hard to tell. But it is accepted that the general route of this trail was followed by these Indians.

Hiking the full length of this trail may be beyond the capabilities of the average backpacker or hiker. Since the distance from Beaver Meadows to Milner Pass is around 14.5 miles, this nearly precludes a one-day round trip. The first part of the trip is 3,000 feet up to Timberline Pass. Camping is possible along the way at Ute Meadow campsite (DD). But, as it is only 2.2 miles up the trail, it is not very centrally located on the hike.

The best way to cover all this trail is to hike it in sections. One recommended starting point is the former site of the so-called Rock Cabins, now a tundra restoration area called Ute Crossing, 2.0 miles past Rainbow Curve on Trail Ridge Road.

There is a parking area about one hundred yards up the road on the left. The trail up, or west, from here is well marked with cairns all along the tundra, and parallels the road most of the way to Milner Pass. Going down, southeast, takes you to Tombstone Ridge and Timberline Pass. This trail section is indistinct, and cairns must be followed. From here drop down to Windy Gulch, past the Ute Meadow campsite, and to the left, along the contours of Beaver Mountain. Toward the end of this section is a fork; the trail to the right leads to the moraine between Beaver Meadows and Moraine Park. Straight ahead a short distance is the picnic and parking area at Beaver Meadows. (The lower part of this trail appears at the top of the Bear Lake/Glacier Gorge map.)

For either route of travel on this trail it will help to have two cars. For instance, on the lower section, one will be left at Beaver Meadows and the other driven to the parking area on Trail Ridge Road, near Ute Crossing. This is a good method to remember on other trails as well, such as the Bear Lake/Fern Lake trailhead hike. If you are without the benefit of two automobiles for such one-way type trails, you can either hitchhike back to your car or turn around and hike back. This is something to consider if you wish to hike the entire trail.

Chapter 10

Across the Divide: The Grand Lake Drainage

GRAND LAKE, NORTH/EAST INLET AREA

From North Inlet trailhead, elevation 8,440 feet, to:

DESTINATION	MILEAGE	ELEVATION (ft.)
Bear Lake	16.0	9,475
Cascade Falls	3.5	8,800
Hallett Creek	10.0	10,620
Lake Nanita	11.0	10,760
Lake Nokoni	10.0	10,760
North Inlet junction	7.5	9,600
North Inlet horse camp	6.5	9,320
Ptarmigan campsite	6.8	9,400
Snow Course campsite	4.3	8,950
Summerland Park	1.0	8,500
From East Inlet trailhead, elevation 8,395 feet, to:		
Adams Falls	0.3	8,450
Boulder-Grand Pass	9.5	12,061
Dipper campsite	5.0	9,640
East Inlet junction	4.5	9,040
Fifth Lake	9.5	10,840
Fourth Lake	8.5	10,360
Gray Jay campsite	5.3	9,760
Lake Verna	7.0	10,160
Lone Pine Lake	5.5	9,880

LAKES AND TRAILS

The Grand Lake drainage region described in this chapter includes Tonahutu Creek, the North Inlet, and the East Inlet. The headwaters of these rivers originate at the continental divide and extend along it from Sprague Mountain, south to the park boundary. This part of Rocky Mountain National Park–the western slope–is a lush, expansive area. It has many campsites, and the greatest number of cross-country camping zones in the park. Hikers and campers staying near Grand Lake have enjoyed this area for years. But, an increasing number of park visitors staying on the Estes Park side are exploring the region as well.

TONAHUTU CREEK TRAIL

The three main rivers in this drainage parallel its three major trails, and draw their names from those rivers. A favorite of many is the Tonahutu Creek trail. Two access points exist for this trail in the immediate vicinity of Grand Lake. One is directly north of the town of Grand Lake on the road to the filtration plant, which, incidentally, is also the North Inlet trailhead. A second is in the vicinity of the Grand Lake ranger station. These trails meet less than a mile up the trail, and continue up the creek to the first of several campsites, Lodgepole (LA), 2.1 miles from the trailhead. From here it is about 1.0 mile to Paint Brush and South Meadows campsites (LG, LH). These sites are just before the huge, open expanse of Big Meadows along Tonahutu Creek. (*Tonahutu* means "big meadow" in Arapaho.) Big Meadows campsite (LB) is located at the junction of the Tonahutu Creek trail and the Green Mountain trail.

From its trailhead on Trail Ridge Road north of Grand Lake, the Green Mountain trail ascends through dense timber for 1.8 miles to Big Meadows. It is the preferred route for reaching the campsites on the Tonahutu trail, with the exception of Lodgepole (LA). By taking the Green Mountain trail, you cut about 2.5 miles off the distance to Big Meadows from the Grand Lake trailhead. The trail follows the edge of Big Meadows on the west. A half-mile after the Green Mountain trail joins the Tonahutu trail, there is a left fork leading to the Onahu Creek trail and its campsites below Long Meadows.

Nearly 3.0 miles past this point, following the Tonahutu Creek trail, is Granite Falls. A short distance above and below this falls are the Granite Falls and Lower Granite Falls campsites (LC, LJ). This is about 5.2 miles up the trail from Green

Mountain trailhead. It is bordered on the north by Nakai Peak and the 1L cross-country zone, and on the south by the 2L cross-country zone around Mount Patterson.

The trail continues past Granite Falls to Tonahutu Meadows (LD), about 1.0 mile away. Another 0.5 mile or so is the Murphy campsite (LK). Murphy is the name of an obscure lake at the base of the north face of Snowdrift Peak, off the right side of the trail. Murphy Lake is accessible by bushwacking up the stream from the Tonahutu trail; but, a climb of over 1,400 feet through steep timber convinces many to leave it unvisited. For those interested, it's just over 1.0 mile. When you reach a small pond surrounded by a meadow, you are halfway to Murphy Lake. From the pond, take the right fork of the creek. The lake lies in a cirque formed by the impressive, 600-foot sheer north face of Snowdrift Peak.

Retrace your route to the Murphy campsite. From there, the trail, which up to this point has mostly been gentle, begins to rise considerably for 0.5 mile to Timberline campsite (LF), the last one on this trail. It sits on the southwest slope of Sprague Mountain, west of the visibly flat area of Bighorn Flats. From this campsite, trips can be made to Haynach Lakes by following the creek up the valley 1.5 miles. Follow the creek past a small lake to the point where it begins to disappear. At this point, go up and over the small ridge on your left. This will bring you to the largest of the Haynach Lakes, most of which are insignificant ponds. The more conventional route into the Haynach Lakes and Haynach campsite (LL) involves leaving the Tonahutu Creek trail between the Murphy and Timberline campsites at the Horse campsite (LE). A trail goes up into the trees on the left side of the trail for about 0.3 mile to the Haynach campsite. You can reach the lakes by following the creek up the fairly gentle valley for another mile. This also makes a good base camp for the ascent of Stones Peak and Sprague Mountain.

The trail rises from Timberline campsite (LF) about 600 feet to the beginning of Bighorn Flats, ultimately ending at Bear Lake. The distance covered in this one-way trip is about 16.0 miles. Add 2.5 miles if you begin or end at Grand Lake. It is wise to initiate this trip at Bear Lake because after the initial 4.4 miles to the top of Flattop, it's downhill the rest of the way. This route is part of a popular Tonahutu/North Inlet circle trip for more experienced backpackers. The distance covered in this two- to three-day trip is 24.5 miles. If you travel this route, you will note signs indicating the danger of unexpected whiteouts from dense cloud cover. In such situations, disorientation can be a real hazard, so take note of the weather.

NORTH INLET TRAIL

The North Inlet can be approached from its trailhead near Grand Lake, or, like the Tonahutu Creek trail, from Bear Lake. Beginning from Grand Lake, the first leg of the trip involves walking the road into Summerland Park for about 1.0 mile, past the campsite there (MA).

After Summerland, the trail begins to rise, and once you enter the forest, it begins snaking back and forth. Cascade Falls and its campsite (MB) are 2.3 miles past the Summerland Park campsite, and 3.5 miles from the trailhead. Right after the Cascade Falls campsite, the trail opens onto a meadow, at the end of which is Snow Course campsite (MC). A cluster of four campsites is found about 2.0 miles past Snow Course, along a beautiful section of trail. The cascading river seemingly creates one grotto after another. These campsites, all within 0.5 mile of each other, are: Grouseberry (MH), North Inlet horse camp (MD), Foot Bridge (MK), and Ptarmigan (ME).

Ptarmigan Creek enters the North Inlet here on your left. Its origin is reached by some very steep hiking up to a hanging valley.* This valley is the location of the Ptarmigan Creek cross-country zone (2M). At the end of this valley are Snowdrift Lake on the southeast slope of Snowdrift Peak, and Ptarmigan Lake, just south of Bighorn Flats. Bench Lake is at the south end of the valley, and just below Bench to the southwest is War Dance Falls. A fishermen's trail—by definition, indistinct—leads to Bench Lake along Ptarmigan Creek from the North Inlet trail. An easier approach to this area is via Flattop Mountain, taking a route directly west, and descending to

*A hanging valley is one that sits above, and on the side of, a more prominent valley. Its name derives from the steep ascent required to reach it. Hanging valleys are common features in glaciated mountains.

Ptarmigan Creek along the drainage from Ptarmigan Pass.

From the Ptarmigan Creek crossing, it is 0.8 mile of steep trail to the North Inlet trail junction and campsite MF. To the right is the trail to Lakes Nokoni and Nanita, 2.4 and 3.5 miles away, respectively. The trail to these lakes crosses the bottom of the valley for a short distance to the North Inlet Falls and campsite MJ. In this vicinity is still another fork. To the left is Pine Marten campsite (ML), 0.2 miles away. One more mile up the river, following closely the trail to the left, is Lake Solitude and the Upper North Inlet cross-country zone (3M), which encompasses the rest of the valley. This trail to Lake Solitude does not appear on the McHenrys Peak (1957) 7.5-minute series map, but is on the larger (1961) park map for this chapter.

From the North Inlet Falls, the trail to Nokoni goes up a series of switchbacks, which cease just before the lake is reached. Lake Nokoni is a scene of classic mountain beauty. The prominent wall on the far side is the north face of Ptarmigan Mountain. Equally beautiful is Lake Nanita, 1.1 miles past Nokoni. The trail veers up through the trees on the east side of Nokoni, and then drops to Nanita. From here, Ptarmigan Mountain is seen from a different, although no less impressive, angle. The glaciated saddle between it and Andrews Peak is above on the right. Camping near Nanita is permitted within the confines of the Upper North Inlet cross-country zone, and compares favorably with any camping area in the park. The round trip to Nokoni and Nanita is 20.0 and 22.0 miles, respectively, so allow enough time to reach these beautiful lakes. Pettingell Lake is over the rise, northwest of Nokoni. Climb directly north up to this small saddle, and then hike down to the west. Pettingell Lake is less than 1.0 mile from Nokoni, and makes either a fine side trip or a destination in itself, as cross-country camping is permitted nearby, in zone 4M.

Let's return now to the main North Inlet trail. Recall that the trail to Nokoni cuts off to the right at the North Inlet junction. Continuing on the North Inlet trail past the junction for about 0.2 mile, you will encounter Hallett Creek and the beginning of a substantial number of switchbacks. These switchbacks are hard work, especially after hiking almost 8.0 miles up from the trailhead. But, once you get above this section, the trail becomes more gentle, as it parallels Hallett Creek. Just over 1.5 miles from the North Inlet junction is the Hallett group site (MG) near the Patrol Cabin. This cabin was built in 1914, prior to the establishment of the park, by the Colorado Mountain Club. The last campsite on this trail, July (MM), is 0.5 mile further.

Since at this point, you are 9.7 miles from the trailhead, you may elect to enter the valley of Hallett Creek from the east, via Flattop Mountain, saving a little over 2.0 miles. However, like the descent into the Ptarmigan Creek area, the descent to Hallett Creek from Flattop is steep. Although you have the benefit of a good switchbacking trail, it is tiring even walking down, and remember that you must hike back up on your return.

The trail from Bear Lake to Grand Lake via the North Inlet trail is 16.0 miles one way, and has for many years been a popular hiking route on a one-way/one-day basis, or as part of a round trip, utilizing the Tonahutu Creek trail. The author is acquainted with one hiking fanatic who completed this round trip in one day. This feat, however, is not recommended for those who consider themselves sane.

EAST INLET TRAIL

The last of the major trails in the Grand Lake drainage is the trail following the East Inlet. Its trailhead is on the east side of Grand Lake near the West Portal of the Alva B. Adams Tunnel. This tunnel is part of a water diversion project to bring western-slope water into the Big Thompson River. It runs under the mountains for over 13.0 miles, and empties at the East Portal near the YMCA camp west of Estes Park. Much of this trail is reminiscent of the North Inlet trail. Both trails follow a river; each passes through lush, if boggy, meadows; and the valleys of both are surrounded by mountains.

At the beginning, the East Inlet trail climbs slightly, but levels out almost immediately, just after the sign for Adams Falls, a short walk to the right. Incidentally, these falls are about one minute away and very impressive to view. Water races down at an amazing rate through deep grottos. If not on the way up, then certainly see them on your way back. Very soon the first open area comes into view, as does the valley of the East Inlet. The mountain, at what appears to be the end of the valley, is Mount Craig. On the left is Mount Cairns, with Mount Wescott to the right. The Mount Enentah cross-country zone (1N) begins near the top of Mount Cairns, and extends north to Mount Enentah, the mountain dividing the North and East Inlets. To give you a visual idea of the distance, the base of Mount Craig is about 4.0 miles from the first meadow and 4.5 miles from the trailhead. The route circles around the meadow and returns to the trees. One and a half miles from the trailhead, you reach the East Meadow campsite (NH), located on the north side of the large second meadow. From here, the trail begins rising perceptibly, and 0.8 mile along is the Lower East Inlet campsite (NA). At this point, the south face of Mount Cairns is visible directly up from the left side of the trail.

For the next mile, the trail, which has been reasonably gradual, begins to climb steeply. At the first true switchback is an exposed outcropping above a set of falls in the river. Unfortunately the lay of the land precludes a view of the falls. This switchback goes up around the outcropping and then levels off again. Shortly thereafter it drops down to the river and Cat's Lair campsite (NJ) at the 4.0-mile mark. Just 0.3 mile further is the East Inlet junction and campsite NB. To the right, along a seldom used trail, is Paradise Park, at the southernmost end of the park. The left fork in the trail leads up more steeply to the Dipper campsite (NC) and Gray Jay (ND), both about 0.5 mile away.

Lone Pine Lake is above these sites an additional 0.5 mile at the 5.5-mile mark. This is the first of a series of lakes in the upper East Inlet. The trail follows the south shore of Lone Pine Lake, and then veers to the left at Solitaire campsite (NE). At this point, the trail goes steeply to the right (east), and then right again, up a very rocky section. At the top of this section, you hit the river's edge once again, and turn left, following it to Lake Verna a mile away. The first site on this magnificent lake is just past a cascade coming down from the

The top of the East Inlet. Fifth Lake is in the valley below. The summit of Isolation Peak is visible above the lake in the center of the photograph. (Photograph by the author.)

north slope of Mount Craig to your right. The first part of the lake you see is a small cove on its western side. It isn't until the first Lake Verna campsite (NF) that you have a full view of the lake. This lake is a favorite spot for fishermen. There are fine places to camp on the west side of Lake Verna. Following a recently improved trail on the left side of the lake, the trail proceeds above Verna to the increasingly poor trail to Spirit Lake. Very often through the summer and well into fall, this section is damp. The spire or protruding rock buttress above these lakes to the south is part of an unnamed mountain between Isolation Peak and Mount Craig. Above it, over the ridge, is Ten Lake Park, a sprinkling of several alpine lakes around 11,000-12,000 feet high.

Upper East Inlet cross-country zone (2N) includes Spirit Lake, and the rest of the forested part of the valley of the East Inlet. Within this zone is also the next lake, appropriately called Fourth Lake. Along the north side of Spirit, a section of trail leads to Fourth Lake, but shortly the trail ends, and you must find your own way, which isn't at all difficult. Climbing up past Fourth Lake, over the meadows at timberline, and following the stream takes you to the final lake in this series, Fifth Lake. Directly south of Fifth Lake is the rugged north face of Isolation Peak. On the other side of this ridge is Moomaw Glacier and Frigid Lake in Wild Basin.

South of the East Inlet trail junction, in the valley of Paradise Park, is Adams Lake, which is fairly inaccessible on the east side of Mount Adams, 12,121 feet. On the right side of the trail leading into Paradise Park is Mount Wescott and the beginning of two contiguous cross-country zones (3N, 1P). This part of the park is visited infrequently. If you want to escape as much as possible, this is a particularly appropriate area in which to camp.

MOUNTAINS OF THE AREA

One distinguishing feature of the Grand Lake drainage is the relative lack of rugged mountains, which, although appealing in an aesthetic sense, is not conducive to climbing. Most of the previously described mountains along the divide are accessible via western slope trails, but because of the distances involved, most routes originate on the eastern slope of the divide. There are exceptions, however, and we shall examine the most notable of these.

PTARMIGAN MOUNTAIN

Ptarmigan Mountain, 12,324 feet, is one of the more impressive on the western slope, especially as seen from the North Inlet trail. The route to Ptarmigan follows up the North Inlet trail and the cutoff to Lake Nokoni. North of this lake, you begin to climb west up to rock and tundra, as you would to reach Pettingell Lake. At the crest of this first ridge, turn left (south) and work toward the main ridge. After the high spot on this ridge, it levels off to a point accessible to the main western flank of Ptarmigan. By following this ridge near the crest of the steep north face, you can reach the summit without difficulty. From here, there is a particularly fine view of both the North and East Inlets. Almost directly west is Mount Enentah, and the 1N cross-country zone to the south. Northwest are Nisa Mountain and the higher Mount Patterson to the right. Two cross-country zones (1M, 2L) are found here.

Andrews Peak from the North Inlet trail. (Photograph by the author.)

ANDREWS PEAK

Andrews Peak, 12,565 feet, which sits southeast of Lake Nanita, can be easily climbed by leaving Ptarmigan and descending southeast to the glaciated ridge between the two peaks. At the bottom of the main summit of Ptarmigan is a small saddle between it and a high point on this ridge. Move around it on the right, remaining about at that same elevation (12,000 to 12,100 feet). Two more saddles are encountered as you approach the summit ridge on the west side of Andrews. Very little up and down climbing is necessary to reach this point. The summit of Andrews Peak is 500 feet up the ridge. Andrews is also accessible from the western side of Verna, but involves a route more than 2,000 feet up in a fairly direct line.

BEAR LAKE TO WILD BASIN

Above the lakes of the upper East Inlet is Boulder-Grand Pass. As you recall from chapter 7, Mount Alice is just north of this pass, and, approached from this direction, is a technically easy climb. Boulder-Grand Pass connects Thunder Lake trail in Wild Basin and the East Inlet trail. There is a great three-day trip, beginning at Bear Lake, over these trails. Take the trail to Flattop and then drop down to the North Inlet. The first night's camp can be anywhere along here, but it's best to cover as many miles as possible toward Grand Lake. The second day, hike to Grand Lake, and proceed over to the East Inlet trailhead by means of your thumb or your feet. Hike up the East Inlet to Lake Verna, and camp there the second night. The third day involves walking to Spirit Lake, and cutting up into the trees on the left. Once at timberline, veer east toward Boulder-Grand Pass. This is not too difficult if you hike at a slow, constant pace. Once at the pass, descend with caution to the scree around Lake of Many Winds, and through the intermittent meadows to Thunder Lake, and the trail once again. It will help to use the two-car method, leaving one at the Wild Basin ranger station, and driving the other to Bear Lake. If two cars are not available you can arrange for a ride, or possibly hitchhike. Round-trip mileage is close to 38.0 miles. Though this trip is possible anytime during the hiking season, the later the better, to avoid damp trails. September is unquestionably the finest time for this rewarding trip.

MOUNT CRAIG

Mount Craig, 12,007 feet, is southwest of Lake Verna, and can be approached from there. As you approach Lake Verna from Lone Pine Lake, you pass a small pond, more a wide spot in the river than a body of water per se. Just afterward, where a creek comes down from the north side of Mount Craig, is a passable ford across the river. Follow the creek up toward what look like imposing cliffs. Just past timberline, cut west up the steep meadows, work your way over the first ridge, and then around slightly to the left to the second and main north ridge. Once on top of this ridge, it levels out considerably, and the summit is to the left, up the tundra. There is one false summit near the true summit.

ADAMS/BRYANT/ACOMA

Mount Adams, 12,121 feet, is a trip to keep in mind if you camp on the eastern side of the 3N or 1P cross-country zones. A stream leaves the lower reaches of the gentle northwest ridge of Mount Adams, and enters Paradise Creek before making a conspicuous left turn up Paradise Park. Follow this drainage up to the ridge of Adams. Near the top of the drainage and the summit ridge is the beginning of the camping zone.

To the east and completely within cross-country zone camping areas is Mount Bryant, 11,034 feet. Although very close to Grand Lake, this is a particularly wild area. South of Bryant and still within the cross-country zone is Mount Acoma, 10,508 feet.

SNOWDRIFT PEAK/NAKAI PEAK

Snowdrift Peak, 12,274 feet, is an easy trip from Bighorn Flats. Hikers camped in the upper Tonahutu Creek area, who elect to make the trip up to Murphy Lake, can reach Snowdrift starting up the ridge on the northeast side of Murphy. As the terrain begins to level, start cutting more and more to the right (south). Pass the small alpine lake in the basin above, and head up. The specific route you take is unimportant.

Nakai Peak, 12,216 feet, can also be climbed by those camped in the upper Tonahutu Creek area. At the Timberline campsite (LF), follow the stream to Haynach Lakes, as previously described. From there go up west and south to the level basin. The more gradual southern end of the basin is the route up to the summit ridge. If you are camped north of Nakai, in the 1K cross-country zone of Upper Onahu Creek, you ascend to the saddle between Nakai and the continental divide. The initial climb to this saddle is steep. Once there, turn right. Along this ridge, there is one significant false summit between you and the top.

Chapter 11

The Never Summer Range and Upper Colorado River Valley

NEVER SUMMER MTS./UPPER COLORADO R. VALLEY

From Phantom Valley parking area, elevation 9,060 feet, to:

DESTINATION	MILEAGE	ELEVATION (ft.)
Box Canyon campsites	5.5	10,460
Ditch Camp No. 3 campsite	4.5	10,180
Grand Ditch via Lulu City	5.8	10,200
Hitchens Gulch	5.5	10,700
La Poudre Pass	7.0	10,180
Lake of the Clouds	6.0	11,430
Little Yellowstone	4.0	10,100
Lulu City	3.0	9,360
Red Mountain trail to Grand Ditch	2.8	10,230
Shipler cabins	1.8	9,220
Shipler Mine	1.5	9,200
Stage Road campsite	4.0	9,550
From La Poudre Pass, elevation 10,175 feet, to:		
La Poudre Pass trail	1.3	10,185
Lake of the Clouds trail	6.3	10,230
Red Mountain trail	8.0	10,235
Skeleton Gulch trail	3.8	10,200
Thunder Pass trail	3.3	10,195

MAJOR TRAILS

The Never Summer Mountains and the Colorado River occupy the western boundary of Rocky Mountain National Park. They can be reached from Estes Park by driving Trail Ridge Road to Kawuneeche Valley and the Colorado River. This part of the Colorado River is commonly referred to as

Part of the Never Summer Range, with Kawuneeche Valley below. The horizontal cut that appears to be a road is an old water diversion project, the Grand Ditch. (Photograph courtesy of the National Park Service.)

the North Fork, a throwback to the days when the Colorado was called the Grand River.

One of the prominent features of the Never Summer Mountains is a man-made water diversion system carved along fourteen miles of the eastern side of this range at about the 10,200 to 10,300-foot level. It is called the Grand Ditch, and was built, one section at a time, in the 1890s by Japanese, Irish, Swedish, and Chinese laborers. The last stretch, from Baker Gulch to Long Draw Reservoir, was completed in 1929. In the initial stages of construction, the laborers used shovels, sledgehammers, and wheelbarrows to move massive quantities of earth and rock, at wages of seventeen cents to one dollar per day. In some ways it's good that the "good old days" are gone.

The North Fork was an area of many homesteads of early pioneers and a couple of mining camps as well. The most no-

This is the site of the former silver camp, Lulu City. Some logs are barely visible at the far left. The Grand Ditch is above, and Lulu Mountain higher up on the left. (Photograph courtesy of the National Park Service.)

table of these camps was Lulu City. A trail leads to the site of this former camp, but all that remains today is mute evidence that cabins once stood there. The history of this town was similar to many other Colorado mining camps. People settled quickly when pay dirt was found, and vanished when the big strike didn't pay off. Later they might reappear at yet another camp where they were supposed to be "pulling it out of the ground in chunks." Only a very few got rich from this era, but it was a grand dream while it lasted.

Lakes in the Never Summer Mountains are for the most part conspicuous by their absence. First glaciers, and later rivers, cut through the rock of these mountains. There is an absence here of terminal and lateral moraines, the "debris piles" of glacial movement, seen on the eastern slope. Thus the sediment necessary for lake formation was not deposited, resulting in fewer lakes.

PHANTOM VALLEY TO GRAND DITCH

The principal trailhead for much of this region is at the Phantom Valley parking area. This is on the west side of Trail Ridge Road, just past the last of the switchbacks below Milner Pass, and 11.0-12.0 miles north of the Grand Lake entrance. The trail leading to Lulu City, 3.0 miles up, starts from the parking area and goes north for about 1.5 miles to Shipler Park and the old Shipler Mine, whose tailings you will cross. The Shipler cabins may be seen 0.3 mile further. The 7.5-minute series, Fall River Pass map (1958) has a few discrepancies regarding trails between Shipler cabins and Lulu City. If you would like to note them on a 7.5-minute map, consult the 80-foot contour interval map in the map section.

Past the Shipler cabins, the trail continues to be gentle and reenters the forest for a short distance before rising along the right side of the canyon. Past Shipler cabins 1.2 miles is a fork in the trail. The left fork leads to Lulu City, 0.2 mile down along the North Fork. The right fork continues at about the same elevation for a while, drops down to the river valley, and then up to meet the Poudre Pass trail and the Stage Road campsite (JE). This campsite is 1.0 mile past the Lulu City cutoff. This particular section of trail, which drops down to the valley toward the campsite, is unmarked on even the chapter map, so simply follow the trail signs in this area.

In the vicinity of campsite JE, there is a trail back to Lulu City, 0.6 mile down. North of the campsite, the trail continues up the valley of the North Fork on the west side, passing by the so-called Little Yellowstone. This is an area of eroded volcanic rock, much of which is yellowish. There are some interesting geologic peculiarities in this region you may want to explore.

From the Stage Road campsite (JE), it is 1.8 miles until you reach the road along the Grand Ditch. From here you can follow the road north for 1.2 miles to La Poudre Pass. La Poudre Pass campsite (JA) is nearby, just inside the park boundary and west of the Grand Ditch. This pass, a feasible trailhead for many hikers in the northern Never Summers, can be reached by driving up Poudre Canyon past Chambers Lake to the Long Draw Road. The road, which passes Long Draw

Reservoir, ends at La Poudre Pass. The total distance from Phantom Valley trailhead to La Poudre Pass is just under 7.0 miles.

From the Stage Road campsite (JE), a trail continues along Lulu Creek. Ditch Camp campsite (JB) is 0.8 mile along this relatively steep trail. It is named after a camp presumably used by the builders of the Grand Ditch at the turn of the century. A short distance above is the ditch itself. On reaching it, turn left and walk a short distance to the sign indicating the trail to Thunder Pass, 1.7 miles away. Just over 0.5 mile on this trail is Box Canyon campsite (JC), located near where Lulu Creek crosses a meadow.

Following the Grand Ditch past the Thunder Pass trail, along the ditch road for 0.5 mile, you will pass an unimproved trail into cross-country zone 1J in Skeleton Gulch. Other camping sites in this region can be reached by following the ditch road south. But the best place to start, in order to reach them, is back at the Phantom Valley trailhead.

LAKE OF CLOUDS

Virtually the only lake in the Never Summers within the park boundary is Lake of Clouds. The name is a reference to the mountains in this range with names like Stratus, Nimbus, Cumulus, and Cirrus. The standard route to the lake is up the Red Mountain trail, which leaves the Phantom Valley trailhead. It runs south and up the side of the valley for about 1.5 miles, and then runs north in a wide switchback for about an equal distance to its junction with the Grand Ditch, 2.8 miles from the trailhead. Following the ditch road north for 1.7 miles, you reach the crossing at Hitchens Gulch and the trail west to Lake of Clouds. This trail ascends near Big Dutch Creek, but soon leaves the creek. Along the first part of the trail you will pass a couple old cabins. One mile above the ditch on a reasonably good, but occasionally damp, trail that passes through several beautiful meadows, is Hitchens Gulch campsite (JD). Above it is the Dutch Town campsite (JF), 0.2 mile away.

The Lake of Clouds trail ends a short distance above Hitchens Gulch campsite, as the trail ascends to a huge boulder-filled basin below Lead Mountain and Mount Cirrus.

Lake of Clouds is above the steep tundra and rock on the left (south) side of the Cirrus ridge, directly west of the end of the trail. To reach the lake, you must pick your way over the boulders, initially heading toward the rocky ridge, and then veering quite a bit to your left. Rock-climbing isn't necessary to reach the lake, but for a short distance some pretty steep hiking is required. It is 5.5 miles to Hitchens Gulch campsite and about 6.0 miles to the lake via the Red Mountain trail.

A shorter alternative route that lacks trail for some of the way is an option for Lake of Clouds hikers. It involves bush-wacking up Big Dutch Creek. Take the trail toward Lulu City until you reach the rock tailings of Shipler Mine, 1.4 miles from Phantom Valley, toward the end of Shipler Park. Shortly afterward drop off the trail to your left and head toward the river through the edge of the forest. In early summer, you may have to cross the river on fallen logs, but it is usually fordable. Locate the Big Dutch Creek inlet, and begin following it up toward the Grand Ditch along the right side of the creek. The route is littered with fallen logs, and, initially, is rather steep. Although the lay of the land makes it unfeasible to walk within sight of the creek, try to stay within hearing range of it. This will bring you to the sharp curve of the ditch road, just north of the Lake of Clouds trail crossing. Assuming an average winter snowfall, this route is impassable in early June. Other than that, this is an interesting and relatively expedient route to the lake.

ALONG THE GRAND DITCH

The remaining campsites of the Never Summer area are south of the Red Mountain trail, along the Grand Ditch. After hiking to the ditch via this trail, 2.8 miles, follow the ditch south to Valley View campsite (JG) on the west side of the road. This campsite is appropriately named, as it offers an excellent view of the valley of the North Fork.

About 0.5 mile further south along the Grand Ditch is the Mosquito Creek campsite (JH). Less than another 0.5 mile you will encounter Opposition Creek campsite (JJ). Both of these sites lie just east of the boundary of the 2J cross-country zone at the lower slopes of Howard Mountain and Mount Cumulus, an area known as Hells Hip Pocket. This part of the

For years Specimen Mountain was thought to be the remnants of an ancient volcano. However, the current theory is that it is the result of lava and ash flow from a volcano miles away. (Photograph courtesy of the National Park Service.)

Never Summers sounds rather hostile if you pay attention to the place-names; but rest assured that, with the possible exception of Mosquito Creek, the connotations are unjustified.

HOLZWARTH CABINS

The Grand Ditch is also accessible via a primitive road (actually a trail) leading up from Holzwarth cabins, at the southern part of this section. This road, which enters the Grand Ditch just outside the park, south of Red Gulch, is an alternative route to campsites along the ditch, though this involves a longer hike. Holzwarth cabins, the main ranch, and much of the upper Kawuneeche Valley have been added to the park since the 1961 map in the map section of this book was made. The Holzwarth cabins have been retained and maintained by the Park Service for historical interest to acquaint visitors with aspects of early pioneer life in the area. A visit to these cabins is most worthwhile. Check with the Estes Park headquarters or Grand Lake ranger station regarding the program at Holzwarth's.

MOUNTAINS OF THE NEVER SUMMER RANGE

SPECIMEN MOUNTAIN

Although not actually in the Never Summer Mountains, Specimen Mountain, 12,489 feet, deserves mention here. It was long thought that Specimen Mountain was an extinct volcano, whose ash flow deposits were evidenced in the vertical rock wall to the west of Iceberg Lake on Trail Ridge Road. These deposits of compacted volcano residue were deep enough to fill whole valleys, such as those at Milner Pass and the Cache La Poudre River. Recently, however, evidence has been found that suggests much of the volcanic deposits of Specimen Mountain came from the vicinity of Lulu Mountain. The main magma caldron that supposedly fed the volcanos of the region 28 million years ago is located near Mount Richthofen, the site of still another, more ancient volcano. It is also interesting that the Arapaho Indian name for Specimen Mountain translated to "Mountain Smokes." Legend has it that some early Indians tried to reach the top to investigate smoke coming from the summit, but had to turn back because the rocks were too hot to walk on.

Today Specimen Mountain is visited by hikers, not in search of strange smoking rock, but for the great view of the Never Summers and the elusive bighorn sheep. Since this area is a habitat for these grand creatures, the Specimen Mountain trail is off limits to hikers from May 1 to July 1, when the lambing season is at a close. The off-limits designation helps protect the sheep from intrusion during this period.

To reach Specimen Mountain, start at the trailhead located along Trail Ridge Road just north of Milner Pass by Poudre Lake. The Specimen Mountain trail begins to rise rather steeply shortly after entering the trees. If you are a beginning hiker, don't be discouraged, for it isn't long before timberline is reached and the trail becomes more gradual: From here the trail proceeds across the tundra to the 1.0-mile mark and a saddle on the lengthy south ridge of the mountain. Below you is a valley, called the Crater, now closed to hikers. Someone incorrectly thought the crater was the mouth of a volcano, probably due to the impressive exposure of layers of volcanic debris northwest of this saddle. From this point—contrary to what is shown on the larger scale, 7.5-minute series map—follow the ridge up to a false summit, and then down and up again to the top of Specimen. (The trail, as shown on the map in the map section, is the correct route.) Although this is a relatively easy mountain to climb, and one often chosen for conditioning hikes, there are still a few things to keep in mind. A vertical rise of more than 1,700 feet is involved in its ascent, much of it over open tundra with no shelter. In such places, it's a good idea to keep your eyes on the weather. In addition, plan to bring your own water, since there is none available enroute to the summit.

Incidentally, the Poudre River trail begins on the northern side of Poudre Lake, toward Fall River Pass on the left side of the road. Five miles away, this connects with the Chapin Creek trail in the vicinity of the Cache campsite (HB). This trail can be boggy in the early part of the summer.

LULU/THUNDER/NEOTA

Lulu Mountain, 12,228 feet, which was part of an ancient volcano system, is one of three mountains clustered along the continental divide in the northern Never Summers. Its two neighbors are Thunder Mountain, 12,020+ feet, and Mount Neota, 11,734 feet. All can be approached from at least three directions. One approach involves driving or hiking to La Poudre Pass via Poudre Canyon. Neota Creek runs from the northwest and empties into Long Draw Creek (formerly La Poudre Pass Creek, as on the 1958 Fall River Pass topographical map) just north of the parking area at the pass. Follow Neota Creek all the way up to a saddle on the north ridge of Thunder Mountain. From there, turn left and walk up the gradual ridge to the summit, a mere 400 feet of easy hiking. From Thunder, Mount Neota is below and to your left, while Lulu Mountain is higher and on your right. Both are accessible along the ridges they share with Thunder Mountain.

A second approach can be made by driving up Poudre Canyon, but continuing over Cameron Pass, and dropping down to the Michigan River Valley. Take the first dirt road on the left to the east 1.0 mile up the valley, past the former site of Willey's Lumber Camp. The hike to Thunder Pass and Michigan Lakes begins at the end of this road. This trail ascends through alternating meadows and forest 800 feet to the Michigan Lakes, with Thunder Pass just above, at the 2.5-mile mark. From the pass, turn left (east), and hike the western ridge of Lulu Mountain. Thunder Mountain and Mount Neota are accessible from here by some summit-ridge traversing.

The third approach is to begin at Phantom Valley trailhead, and take the previously described trail to Lulu City, the Grand Ditch, and up to Thunder Pass.

MOUNT RICHTHOFEN

Mount Richthofen, 12,940 feet, is the highest mountain in the Never Summer Range, and is frequently climbed by beginning at Phantom Valley trailhead. Take the trail to Thunder Pass. When you reach the Grand Ditch, walk along the ditch about 0.3 mile up to a meadow that opens to the left. Turn west through the meadow and begin ascending. It is rather steep going initially, but will become easier as you reach the top of this eastern ridge. Continue along the tundra on this ridge dividing Skeleton Creek and Box Canyon toward the prominent eastern slopes of Richthofen. As you approach the steeper area of the mountain, there is a prominent rock face jutting out on the southeastern side. Skirt this rock face on the right, and head up the final section en route to the summit.

Mount Richthofen is also accessible from the west and north by hiking to Lake Agnes, located outside the park boundary. Drive over Cameron Pass on Colorado Route 14 from Fort Collins. The route to Lake Agnes begins at a Colorado state forest trailhead, the former site of Willey's Lumber Camp, as previously described. From Lake Agnes, traverse around the west edge of the lake and up the boulder-strewn couloir to the saddle on the west ridge of Richthofen. From here, the route steepens and goes east, up toward the summit. Again, be cautious of the scree and loose rock. The last short pitch to the top is along a somewhat exposed ridge, and it is advised to stay on, or just north of, the top until you reach the summit.

STATIC PEAK/TEPEE MOUNTAIN

Static Peak, 12,560+ feet, and Tepee Mountain, 12,360 feet, are Richthofen's northern and southern neighbors, respectively. Both can be reached by first climbing Richthofen. It is unusual for them to be ascended without taking in Richthofen as well. Static Mountain is to the north, along a ridge of loose rock approximately 0.5 mile. One-half mile south along another ridge of loose rock is Tepee Mountain. This trip is not recommended unless you are prepared to return almost all the way back up to the summit of Richthofen for a similar return route. The average hiker will be unable to descend back toward the Grand Ditch without encountering some technically difficult situations. The rock all over this area of the Never Summers is very unstable. Since the scree slopes are filled with loose, sharp-edged rock, caution is advised on any steep slope in this range.

HOWARD/CIRRUS/LEAD

Howard Mountain, 12,810 feet, Mount Cirrus, 12,797 feet, and Lead Mountain, 12,537 feet, are a trio of mountains grouped roughly in the geographical center of the Never Summer Range. The approach for all three begins at the Phantom Valley trailhead. The Red Mountain trail, up to the Grand Ditch, is the best route to Howard Mountain. Once at the Grand Ditch, turn south and walk down to the bridge crossing at Mosquito Creek campsite (JH). Begin ascending to timberline along the banks of this creek. When you reach timberline, start veering to the right a bit. A short distance away is a relatively flat shelf, on which sits the unobtrusive Pinnacle Pool. Pick your way over the slabs of rock past this small lake, and begin ascending the valley below Howard Mountain. The route lies up the steep ridge of the continental divide directly at the head of this valley. Since some steep snow may be encountered earlier in the year, an ice ax may be of some value. After you have switchbacked your way up, the summit of Howard Mountain is north, to the right, and up 400 feet.

Mount Cirrus can be easily reached about 0.5 mile along the ridge north from Howard. The descent from Howard Mountain or Mount Cirrus is easily accomplished by returning via Lake of Clouds. From the saddle between the two mountains, begin picking your way down the steep tundra, and around some boulders en route to the lake, nearly 1,000 feet below. Once at the lake, move around the south edge of the lake to the flat tundra along the east bank. From there go east, dropping over the shelf on which the lake sits, and descend over another, but much shorter, stretch of steep rock and tundra. Bear to the left and head east as you descend, before hitting the trees, so you can locate the trail back to the Grand Ditch. You can return to Phantom Valley either back along the Grand Ditch to the Red Mountain trail, or by descending without trail along Dutch Creek as previously described. Incidentally, Mount Cirrus and Howard Mountain can be ascended by this return route. But if you choose to climb these mountains via the Lake of Clouds, it might be a good idea to camp the evening before at Hitchens Gulch.

To ascend Lead Mountain, take the route via Hitchens Gulch, as though you were going to Lake of Clouds. But, just below the shelf of the lake at timberline, veer to the north across a huge boulder field. Directly north is an elongated ridge projecting east from the summit of Lead. The summit is on the continental divide ridge itself, as are virtually all the mountains of the Never Summer Range. Climb to the saddle between Lead Mountain and the "summit" of its eastern ridge. Here, too, caution is advised due to the scree and generally loose rock. From the saddle, turn west and head up along the left side of the summit ridge, keeping below the crest until just before you reach the summit. Return the same way.

It is best to camp at Hitchens Gulch or Dutch Town campsites (JD, JF) the night before climbing Lead, Howard, or Cirrus, especially if you intend to climb more than one peak in a day. This is also a pleasant area of the park to pitch a tent.

CUMULUS/NIMBUS/STRATUS/BAKER

Mount Cumulus, 12,725 feet, Mount Nimbus, 12,706 feet, Mount Stratus, 12,520+ feet, and Mount Baker, 12,397 feet, are the southernmost mountains of the Never Summer Range. The principal approach route for Mount Cumulus begins, once again, at the Phantom Valley trailhead. Follow the Red Mountain trail to the Grand Ditch, and then turn left (south) and follow the road to Opposition Creek campsite (JJ). Cross the ditch and head up through the thick timber along Opposition Creek. As timberline approaches, veer north and begin the ascent of Cumulus's southeast ridge. Follow the crest of this ridge west to the continental divide, and then north to the summit. Practically no route-finding is required for this ascent. Cumulus is one of the more gradual mountains of this range.

Since Mount Nimbus and Mount Stratus are close together, separated only by a short, comparatively easy section of ridge, they are often climbed together. Follow Opposition Creek to timberline, as with Mount Cumulus, but continue up the drainage instead of heading north to the saddle north of Nimbus. Once on the ridge (the continental divide), turn south and follow it up to the summit of Nimbus, about 650 feet above. The summit of Mount Stratus is less than 0.5 mile south along the ridge. Green Knoll stands out as the high point of the eastern ridge of Mount Stratus. Likewise, Red Mountain, 11,605 feet, is a prominence on the far end of an elongated ridge, east of Mount Nimbus. These last two are less interesting ascents than those of the more prominent peaks.

The southernmost mountain in the Never Summer Range is Baker Mountain. It can be climbed as part of a trip to Nimbus and Stratus by continuing the southerly ridge traverse from Stratus. But, if you are headed only for Baker Mountain, the best approach is to begin at Holzwarth Cabins. From there, walk up the access road to the Grand Ditch, turn to the left, and walk along the ditch for just over a mile. Along the southern slope of Baker is a large area of rock and sparse vegetation. Cross the ditch, which normally is not very difficult, and head up. The route is fairly direct with no special problems. It is, however, one that requires patience, conditioning, and a lot of switchbacking. The summit is only 0.5 mile away from the ditch road, but 2,000 feet higher.

Incidently, Baker Gulch, which is outside the park boundaries on the west side of Baker Mountain, is a fine place to camp. It also serves as a good base camp for climbing Mount Nimbus, Mount Stratus, and Baker Mountain, via Baker Pass or directly. Although Baker Gulch is outside the park in Arapaho National Forest, it may be wise to check with the backcountry office on any regulations that may affect camping there.

One final reminder is in order for mountaineers in the Never Summers. The rock in this range is not the good solid granite found in the rest of the park. Any ridge-traversing or steep angle ascents are cause for concern. Ascend loose rock in close formation. Keep your eyes open for hikers above you who may carelessly knock rocks down, and for those below you, who are depending on your good sense of safety.

Appendix A

DESIGNATED BACKCOUNTRY CAMPSITES

On the following pages are the designated campsite locations, with references to maps in the map section. The site names often refer to nearby geographic features on the park topographic maps. These campsites may be changed or closed at specific areas. Many of the higher elevation campsites are not available for camping in June, and some of the campsites may be limited to "stoves only" as the season progresses. Any questions concerning park regulations should be resolved before starting up the trail. For specific locations, consult the maps at the beginning of the Trail Guide section. Keep in mind that campsites are occasionally eliminated in favor of new ones. This list is up-to-date at the time of publication, but may not reflect recent changes in backcountry management.

EAST DISTRICT

Code	Site Name	Individual Sites	Group Sites	Mileage from Trailhead
AA	Stormy Peaks*	4	1	11.0
BA	Lost Lake*	4		10.0
BB	Lost Meadow*	3	1	8.5
BC	Halfway	2		5.3
BD	Stormy Peaks South*	2		8.5
BE	Lost Falls	2		6.8
BF	Happily Lost	2		6.3
BG	Aspen Meadow	2		6.0
BH	Silvanmere	2		5.8
BJ	Kettle Tarn	2		5.0
CA	Lawn Lake	4		6.3
CB	Tileston Meadows*	2		6.0
CC	Ypsilon Creek	2		2.3
CD	Roaring River	2		1.5
CE	Big Rock*	2		5.3
CF	Cut Bank group site		1	2.3
CG	Lower Tileston Meadows*	2		6.3
DA	Odessa Lake*	3		4.0
DB	Fern Lake	4	1	3.8
DC	Spruce Lake*	2		4.5
DD	Ute Meadow*	1		6.3
DE	The Pool	3		1.8
DF	Cub Creek*	2		2.3

EA	Boulder Field*	10		6.0
EB	Boulder Brook*	2	1	3.5
EC	Glacier Gorge 1 & 2*	2		3.5
ED	Lake of Glass*	2		4.3
EE	Mill Creek Basin	4		1.5
EF	Upper Wind River*	2		2.3
EG	Over the Hill*	1		2.3
EH	Wind River Bluff*	1		3.0
EJ	Marigold Pond*	2		2.3
FA	Jims Grove*	10		3.0
FB	Battle Mountain group*		1	3.0
FC	Goblins Forest*	6		1.3
FD	Moore Park	2	1	2.0
GA	Sandbeach Lake*	4	1	4.3
GB	Thunder Lake*	4	1	6.8
GC	Bluebird Lake*	2		6.0
GD	Pear Lake*	2		6.5
GE	Hunters Creek	3		3.3
GF	North Saint Vrain	3		3.5
GG	Ouzel Lake*	4		5.0
GH	Pear Creek	3		6.5
GJ	Campers Creek	1		2.3
GK	Ouzel Falls*	4		2.8
GL	Finch Lake	4	1	4.5
GM	Pine Ridge	2		2.5
	Total sites, East District (48 areas)	133	9	

WEST DISTRICT

Code	Site Name	Individual Sites	Group Sites	Mileage from Trailhead
HA	Hague Creek*	2	1	7.0
HB	Cache	2		3.5
HC	Mummy Pass Creek	2		3.8
HD	Koenig*	2		10.5
HE	Chapin group site		1	3.0
JA	La Poudre Pass*	4		8.0
JB	Ditch Camp No. 3	3	1	3.5
JC	Box Canyon*	2		2.8
JD	Hitchens Gulch	2		5.5
JE	Stage Road	2		3.0
JF	Dutch Town*	3		5.5
JG	Valley View*	2		3.0
JH	Mosquito Creek*	2		3.0
JJ	Opposition Creek*	2		3.3
JK	Red Gulch		1	5.0

KA	Timber Creek	2		3.0
KB	Jackstraw	3		4.0
KC	Rockslide	1		4.5
KD	Snowbird	2		4.5
KE	Onahu Creek	2		2.5
KF	Upper Onahu	2		2.8
KG	Onahu Bridge	2		3.0
LA	Lodgepole	2		1.8
LB	Big Meadows*	2	1	2.3
LC	Granite Falls	2		5.3
LE	Tonahutu horse camp		1	6.3
LD	Tonahutu Meadows*	2		6.9
LF	Timberline*	1		7.3
LG	Paint Brush	2		2.3
LH	South Meadows	1		2.5
LJ	Lower Granite Falls	2		5.3
LK	Murphy	2		6.7
LL	Haynach*	2		1.3
MA	Summerland Park	3	1	3.5
MB	Cascade Falls*	2		4.3
MC	Snow Course*	2		6.5
MD	North Inlet horse camp		1	6.3
ME	Ptarmigan	2		6.8
MF	North Inlet Junction	3		7.5
MG	Hallett group site		1	9.3
MH	Grouseberry	2		6.3
MJ	North Inlet Falls	2		7.5
MK	Foot Bridge	3		6.5
ML	Pine Marten	2		7.8
MM	July	3		9.8
NA	Lower East Inlet	2		2.3
NB	East Inlet Junction	1		4.3
NC	Dipper	1		4.8
ND	Gray Jay	1		5.0
NE	Solitaire	1		5.5
NF	Lake Verna	3		7.0
NG	Junco		1	5.0
NH	East Meadow	2		1.5
NJ	Cats Lair*	3		4.0
	Total sites, West District (54 areas)	100	10	

*These campsites are limited to stoves only, meaning camping stoves using white gas, propane, alcohol, etc. Burning of wood, charcoal, and trash is not allowed.

Appendix B

PRINCIPAL MOUNTAINS OF THE PARK

Though the mileages to the summits of the following mountains are approximations and vary according to the route chosen, this is a reasonable guide to distance traveled. This appendix reflects the distances from conventional trailheads, as well as alternate starting points. Alternate trailheads are noted when, because of frequency of use, they warrant mention.

PRINCIPAL MOUNTAINS OF THE PARK

Mountain	Elevation (ft.)	Mileage	Trailhead
Adams, Mt.	12,121	8.0	East Inlet
Alice, Mt.	13,310	9.5	Wild Basin
Andrews Peak	12,565	13.0	North Inlet
Arrowhead	12,387	5.5	Glacier Gorge Junction
Baker, Mt.	12,397	4.5	Holzwarth Cabins
Chapin, Mt.	12,454	1.5	Chapin Creek trailhead
Chiefs Head Peak	13,597	8.5	Wild Basin & Glacier Gorge Junction
Chiquita, Mt.	13,069	2.5	Chapin Creek trailhead
Cirrus, Mt.	12,797	6.0	Phantom Valley parking area
Copeland, Mt.	13,176	7.5	Wild Basin
Cracktop	12,760+	7.5	Timber Lake trailhead & Milner Pass
Craig, Mt.	12,007	8.0	East Inlet
Cumulus, Mt.	12,725	5.0	Phantom Valley parking area
Desolation Peaks	12,949	5.0	Chapin Creek trailhead
Dickinson, Mt.	11,831	11.0	Lawn Lake trailhead
Dunraven, Mt.	12,571	8.5	Lawn Lake trailhead & North Fork trail access
Eagles Beak	12,200+	9.3	Wild Basin (via Thunder Lake)
Estes Cone	11,006	2.5	Longs Peak ranger station
Fairchild Mtn.	13,502	8.8	Lawn Lake trailhead
Fall Mtn.	12,258	4.8	Pingree Park (via Mummy Pass)
Flatiron Mtn.	12,335	6.0	Chapin Creek trailhead
Flattop Mtn.	12,324	4.5	Bear Lake
Gabletop Mtn.	11,939	7.0	Bear Lake

Hagues Peak	13,560	9.0	Lawn Lake trailhead
Hallett Peak	12,713	5.0	Bear Lake
Howard Mtn.	12,810	6.0	Phantom Valley parking area (via Lake of Clouds)
Ida, Mt.	12,880+	6.5	Timber Lake trailhead & Milner Pass
Isolation Peak	13,118	9.3	Wild Basin trailhead
Jackstraw Mtn.	11,704	5.0	Timber Lake trailhead
Julian, Mt.	12,928	8.0	Timber Lake trailhead & Milner Pass
Knobtop Mtn.	12,331	6.3	Bear Lake
Lady Washington, Mt.	13,281	4.8	Longs Peak ranger station
Little Matterhorn	11,586	5.5	Fern Lake parking area & Bear Lake
Longs Peak	14,256	8.5	Longs Peak ranger station, Glacier Gorge Junction
Lead Mtn.	12,537	7.3	Phantom Valley parking area
Lulu Mtn.	12,228	7.0	Phantom Valley parking area, La Poudre Pass via Long Draw
Mahana Peak	12,632	9.0	Wild Basin trailhead
McHenrys Peak	13,327	7.0	Glacier Gorge Junction
Meeker, Mt.	13,911	6.8	Copeland Lake in Wild Basin, Longs Peak ranger station
Mummy Mtn.	13,425	8.5	Lawn Lake trailhead
Nakai Peak	12,216	9.0	Tonahutu Creek trailhead
Neota, Mt.	11,730	7.5	Phantom Valley parking area, La Poudre Pass
Nimbus, Mt.	12,706	5.0	Phantom Valley parking area
Notchtop Mtn.	12,129	5.8	Bear Lake
Orten, Mt.	11,724	5.5	Wild Basin trailhead
Otis Peak	12,486	6.0	Bear Lake, Glacier Gorge Junction
Ouzel Peak	12,716	8.3	Wild Basin trailhead
Pagoda Mtn.	12,497	7.8	Copeland Lake (via Sandbeach trail), Glacier Gorge Junction
Ptarmigan Mtn.	12,324	11.5	North Inlet

Powell Peak	13,208	8.8	Bear Lake
Red Mtn.	11.605	4.0	Phantom Valley parking area
Richthofen, Mt.	12,940	7.8	Phantom Valley parking area (via Lake Agnes trail)
Rowe Mtn.	13,184	10.0	Lawn Lake trailhead
Rowe Peak	13,400	9.5	Lawn Lake trailhead
Shadow Mtn.	10,155	4.5	via Outlet trail (SW shore of Grand Lake)
Snowdrift Peak	12,274	8.0	Bear Lake & Tonahutu Creek trailhead
Specimen Mtn.	12,429	8.3	Milner Pass & Poudre Lake
Spearhead, The	12,575	6.5	Glacier Gorge Junction
Sprague Mtn.	12,713	9.5	Bear Lake
Static Peak	12,560	8.3	Phantom Valley parking area (via Lake Agnes trail)
Stones Peak	12,922	10.8	Bear Lake
Storm Peak	13,326	7.0	Longs Peak ranger station, Glacier Gorge Junction
Stormy Peaks	12,148	5.0	Pingree Park (via the North Fork trail)
Stratus, Mt.	12,520+	5.5	Phantom Valley parking area
Sugarloaf Mtn.	12,120+	5.5	Pingree Park (via North Fork trail)
Tanima Peak	12,420	8.8	Wild Basin trailhead
Taylor Peak	13,153	7.5	Bear Lake
Tepee Mtn.	12,360	8.3	Phantom Valley parking area (via Lake Agnes trail)
Terra Tomah, Mt.	12,718	8.8	Timber Lake trailhead at Milner Pass
Thatchtop Mtn.	12,668	5.5	Glacier Gorge Junction
Thunder Mtn.	12,040	7.8	Phantom Valley parking area, La Poudre Pass
Twin Sisters	11,428	3.5	On Colorado Route 7, Tahosa Valley
Ypsilon Mtn.	12,514	3.5	Chapin Creek trailhead

Bibliography

Andresen, Steve. *The Orienteering Book.* Mountain View, Calif.: World Publications, 1977.

Arps, Louisa Ward, and Kingery, Elinor Eppich. *High Country Names.* Denver: The Colorado Mountain Club, 1966.

Cargo, David and Chisolm, Richard M. *Outdoorsman's Guide to Rocky Mountain National Park.* Boulder: Johnson Publishing Co., 1966.

Ferber, Peggy, ed. *Mountaineering, The Freedom of the Hills.* Seattle: The Mountaineers, 1960.

Fricke, Walter. *Climber's Guide to Rocky Mountain National Park.* Boulder: Published by author, 1971.

Hicks, Dave. *Estes Park from the Beginning.* Denver: Egan Printing Co. and A-T-P Publishing Co., 1976.

Kjellstrom, Bjorn. *Be Expert with Map and Compass.* New York: Charles Scribner's Sons, 1955.

Manning, Harvey. *Backpacking, One Step at a Time.* Seattle: REI Press, 1972.

Nelson, Ruth Ashton. *Plants of Rocky Mountain National Park.* Rocky Mountain Nature Association, Inc., 1976.

Nesbit, Paul W. *Longs Peak, Its Story and Climbing Guide.* Boulder: Johnson Publishing Co., 1972.

Ormes, Robert. *Guide to the Colorado Mountains.* Chicago: The Swallow Press, Inc., 1970.

Richmond, Gerald. *Raising the Roof on the Rockies.* Rocky Mountain Nature Association, Inc., 1974.

Toll, Oliver. *Arapahoe Names and Trails, A Report of a 1914 Pack Trip.* Published by author, Library of Congress No. 62-22215, 1962.

Wegemann, Carroll H. *A Guide to the Geology of Rocky Mountain National Park.* Washington: U.S. Government Printing Office, 1955.

Wilkerson, Dr. James A. *Medicine for Mountaineering.* Seattle: Vail-Ballou Press, 1967.

Willard, Bettie, and Harris, Chester O. *Alpine Wildflowers of Rocky Mountain National Park.* Rocky Mountain Nature Association, Inc. 1963.

Index

ABOUT THE AUTHOR

Erik Nilsson became interested in hiking in Rocky Mountain National Park at age seven, when he and his family were guests at Stead's Ranch in 1956. He returned to the park each summer thereafter, and came to Colorado to stay in 1966, when he entered Colorado State University to study history. His summers were spent working at Wind River Ranch near Estes Park and camping when time permitted. He is a charter member of the Larimer County Mountain Rescue Team in Fort Collins and has worked as a mountaineering store manager, ski instructor, forest fire fighter, and emergency medical technician. Erik Nilsson shares his love for the mountains of Rocky Mountain National Park with the thousands who have for years called the Estes Park area a second home.